REGINA WONG

MAKE
SPACE

A MINIMALIST'S GUIDE TO THE GOOD
AND THE EXTRAORDINARY

Skyhorse Publishing

Skyhorse Publishing books may be purchased in bulk at special discounts for sales promotion, corporate gifts, fund-raising, or educational purposes. Special editions can also be created to specifications. For details, contact the Special Sales Department, Skyhorse Publishing, 307 West 36th Street, 11th Floor, New York, NY 10018 or info@skyhorsepublishing.com.

Skyhorse® and Skyhorse Publishing® are registered trademarks of Skyhorse Publishing, Inc.®, a Delaware corporation.

Visit our website at www.skyhorsepublishing.com.

10 9 8 7 6 5 4 3 2 1

Library of Congress Cataloging-in-Publication Data is available on file.

Cover design by Jenny Zemanek
Cover photo credit: iStockphoto

Print ISBN: 978-1-5107-2141-8
Ebook ISBN: 978-1-5107-2142-5

Printed in the United States of America

Table of Contents

Dedicated to my mom,
and to all that is essential to my happiness.

Introduction

Most books are about more—having more and doing more. This one is about less—how one can live well and better with less. That is, less stuff but the *right* stuff. It is about how minimalism and living more simply can transform your life and help you make the most of it. This book is not just about getting rid of stuff and clutter; it is also about changing your mindset and looking at life with a new perspective. It is a guide to transforming your life in a holistic way.

The fact that you are reading this book points to a need. A need for more happiness, better mental and emotional well-being, more clarity and control over your life's purpose, and greater fulfillment. Contrary to general belief, the meeting of these needs lies not so much in adding more to your life but rather in having less. Most of us have been programmed to think that in order to be happier and to make the most out of our life, we need to have more money, more possessions, more gadgets, more friends, bigger houses and cars, bigger job titles . . . The list of "bigger is better" goes on.

If this were indeed the case, we should be talking about making more money, consuming more, aiming for the next big promotion, and singing the praises of retail "therapy." Doing all of these gives us a little high, but before long, a feeling of emptiness and dissatisfaction sets in once more, and we look again to having even more as the route to happiness. The cycle repeats itself—the high moments get shorter and more stuff is needed to sustain them and satiate us.

Greater wealth, material consumption, and more choices have not made us any happier compared to our grandparents' time, when people owned and owed less. Rather than rising levels of well-being, we have seen mounting credit card debt and increasing numbers of self-storage facilities to house the things that we compulsively buy.

"Compared with their grandparents, today's young adults have grown up with much more affluence, slightly less happiness and much greater risk of depression and assorted social pathology," notes Hope College psychologist David G. Myers, PhD, author of the article, "The funds, friends, and faith of happy people," which appeared in the *American Psychologist*.

"Our becoming much better off over the last four decades has not been accompanied by one iota of increased subjective well-being."

Life is too short for such short-term remedies; we need a cure, not a Band-Aid. We need something that provides us with a holistic and long-term solution. Minimalism can be that solution.

Minimalism is not a deprivation, but a joy. It is about getting rid of excess and the nonessentials, and the act of distilling to what is essential—that which gives us joy, value, and purpose to our lives. It is a practice in evaluating what the constituents of our happiness are and focusing on these essentials for optimal fulfillment. We are not just talking about decluttering the excess physical stuff; we are also talking about our mental and emotional states and how they can be improved. We are looking at achieving a change in our mindset and perspective and creating new habits to bring about a positive and holistic transformation in our life.

A little about myself

So, who am I to tell you that minimalism works? I write a popular blog on minimalism and simple living at *Simple and Minimal* (simpleandminimal.com). I also run my own businesses, including Live Well With Less (livewellwithless. com), which focuses on helping others live happier and fuller lives through minimalism. In addition, I also head up The Minimalists London Meetup Group, which provides friend-ship and support to both aspiring and experienced minimalists through social media and various meetup events.

In my previous life, like many, I was also on a success- and consumption-driven journey, but I found little joy and satisfaction. Minimalism has transformed my life, and I believe it can transform yours, too.

After university, I spent many years as a corporate warrior in the telecoms industry, with stints in Asia and America before returning to the UK. At first, the money and prestige that my career brought me gave me much joy and purchasing power. Whenever I felt unhappy and stressed, all I needed to do was go for retail therapy. There were quite a few occasions when I liked a piece of clothing, couldn't decide which color to buy it in, and so bought them all (it makes me cringe just to think about it now!). As the years went by, I worked harder, traveled more, and earned greater sums of money. Incomprehensibly, I felt unhappier, emptier, more stressed, and increasingly frustrated. Weekends became sacred, as these were the only two days I actually felt happy and in control of my life, and they were for doing my favorite things—like browsing in my favorite bookshops and buying books I hardly had time to read. In a nutshell, I only truly lived two out of seven days in a week, and I was not happy.

In my darkest hour, I realized that I have other options in life. I didn't have to work at a job I hated that didn't align with my values and passions. I could pursue my interests and make a living out of them. I didn't have to live a life I dreaded in order to look forward to retirement (which is not guaranteed for all post–baby boomer generations!). I didn't need the "stuff" that kept me rooted in a life and job that sucked out joy, hope, and energy.

Instead of subscribing to conventional beliefs and benchmarks, I could define how I want to live my life and what makes it "successful." I realized that by reorienting myself to the right priorities, by making different but better choices, and by living with less, I could live life with more freedom, awareness, fulfillment, and intensity. I am now living more—with less. If you have not found what you are looking for with more, why not embrace less and see what it has to offer?

Genuine happiness can only be achieved when we transform our way of life from the unthinking pursuit of pleasure to one committed to enriching our inner lives, when we focus on "being more" rather than simply having more.

—Daisaku Ikeda

Chapter 1:
The Heart of Minimalism

What is minimalism?

When you think of the word *minimalism*, what comes to mind? Monotone clothing? Stark white decor? Near empty spaces? Minimalism can be all of these and a lot more. It is not just a physical manifestation; it is relevant to your mental and emotional levels as well. To get the most out of minimalism, it should be looked at from a holistic perspective and not just a physical one.

Minimalism is really all about reassessing your priorities so that you can strip away the excess and nonessential stuff—the possessions, beliefs, behavior, habits, relationships, and activities—that don't bring value to your life, and focus on the essential stuff that does.

Minimalism is both personal and individual in its definition and practice. There is no benchmark to dictate that you must own a maximum number of belongings, live in a particular type of space, or adopt a particular lifestyle in order to qualify as a minimalist. There is no all or nothing. Minimalism comes in many different hues, and no two minimalists are exactly alike, but their ultimate goal is the same. What unites and defines them is a common set of beliefs, ethos, and practices. For me, these include:

* Keeping only what adds happiness, value, purpose, and freedom to our lives and discarding the rest that is non-essential. This includes both physical (for example, clothes and paperwork) and nonphysical stuff (for example, negative relationships, feelings of worry and stress, unproductive habits, and nonessential commitments).
* Focusing on what we simply cannot live without, rather than asking how little we can live with. Living minimally should be a joy and not a deprivation.
* Being more conscious and mindful of the things, people, experiences, and situations in our lives, so that we live life with more intention, purpose, and intensity.

Minimalism at a personal level is best described by the Swedish word *lagom*. Lagom is defined as "enough, sufficient, adequate, just right." It is also widely translated as "in moderation," "in balance," "perfect-simple," and "suitable." Notice there are no connotations here of an insufficiency that leads to deprivation and certainly no excess that results from over-consumption. Minimalism is like pouring tea into a cup. Too little tea will fail to satiate a need (thirst), and too much will result in an overflowing cup that requires time and effort to clean up.

A common misperception about minimalism and simplicity is that if you have very little or nothing, you are living life as a minimalist. Some people might say, "I have never had much money and don't own many possessions, so I guess I am a minimalist." It is possible that this is true, but minimalism is more about living intentionally and consciously than being financially poor and owning few possessions. It should be a conscious choice rather than something forced upon us.

The focus of minimalism should not be on stuff as much as intention. Some of us might live with few possessions, as it is appropriate for our lifestyle and needs; others might find that their library of three hundred books provides much joy and inspiration. If you love books, getting rid of all your books would probably make you very unhappy, and that defeats the whole premise of minimalism. Minimalism should be about focusing on what is essential to our happiness and fulfillment.

There is a limit, both physical and emotional, that possessions and nonessential stuff can provide us. Buying a $100,000 house might make us very happy. Buying a $500,000 house would not necessarily make us five times happier. This is due to the law of diminishing returns. After a certain point, additional income and possessions do not deliver a significant and corresponding change to our level of happiness; in fact, in many cases, the result is less happiness. Similarly, fewer possessions do not mean less satisfaction. Having less, but having the right stuff, can deliver more fulfillment.

As with most desires and endeavors in life, the ultimate goal or destination is the achievement of happiness. There are many routes and options toward happiness—clearing the clutter in all areas of your life and living minimally by focusing on the essentials helps you to see the road clearer and achieve your goal in a shorter time. At its core, minimalism is an ethos, with a focus on joy and purpose. It is a tool that helps us gain freedom—freedom from being overwhelmed, from nonessential stuff, from consumer culture, from mental clutter, from emotional blockages and negative relationships, from debt and joyless pursuits. It facilitates tangible freedom and the living of an extraordinary life.

Moderation, a balance between less and more, unmeasurable and personal in its definition, is at the heart of minimalism.

—Anonymous

How minimalism can transform your life

Minimalism and living with less is much more than just decluttering our unwanted possessions and stuff. Much of what we carry through life that holds us back from living optimally is not, in fact, stuff or physical objects. Hence, this book is about more than just getting rid of physical stuff. To bring about a significant and fundamental change in your life to achieve the happiness and fulfillment you crave, we also need to look at the nonphysical stuff. This includes limiting mental and emotional beliefs or impediments, such as low confidence, fear of changes and failure, stress, unfulfilling relationships and work, unhealthy addictions, financial debt, and other baggage that impedes living our life to its fullest potential.

Minimalism and living well with less is about having more of the things that matter and less of those that don't. It frees us up to pursue our life's purpose and dreams, increases our options to pursue things that fulfill us, and improves the quality of our lives. It gives us the space to breathe, time to reflect and ponder, and the energy and resources to pursue the things that add value.

The best way to determine what's essential to our life is to review what we cannot live without. To live optimally, we must ask what it is that we want to be and to achieve in our life. Anything that doesn't contribute toward that goal is nonessential. Basically, we are subtracting anything that does not add value or serve a purpose. Through living with less, we sharpen our focus on what's essential, lighten our load, and enjoy the freedom to truly *be*.

This is how my life has changed for the better since I embraced minimalism:

- Enjoying a true sense of freedom with little or nothing to hold me back
- Being more intentional
- Owning fewer possessions—I only have stuff that is essential and that adds value and joy
- Having more mindful consumption
- Reducing my expenses
- Becoming debt-free
- Growing as an individual
- Discovering a purpose and mission in my life
- Only doing things that inspire and fulfill me
- Pursuing interests that align with my passions, values, and financial goals
- Learning to go with the flow

- Learning to let go of the past, appreciate the present, and look forward to the future
- More conscious allocation of time and resources
- Focusing on relationships and activities that support and energize me
- Finding ways to contribute beyond myself

The three factors below have also contributed to my growing interest in minimalism and its benefits:

- The overload on our senses caused by possessions, information, and commitments
- Technological improvements and multifunctions of new equipment (for example, the smartphone and the e-reader) has reduced the stuff we need
- Major financial crashes (such as the one in 2008), natural disasters, and other life-changing events that prompt us to evaluate our priorities

Activity: Can you list five things that you want to achieve by living a more minimalist life?

Question: How do you carve an elephant?

Answer: You get a very large block of stone and chip away everything that does not look like an elephant.

Question: How do you create the life you want?

Answer: You define for yourself what that life would be and then get rid of anything and everything that doesn't contribute to it . . . because all that stuff is clutter!

—Kate Carpenter

Can I be a minimalist?

The answer to that is: "Yes, of course!" Minimalists come from all demographics, nationalities, and backgrounds. One is never too young or too old to start the journey. I used to think: *How I wish I had discovered minimalism earlier!* But I came to the conclusion that it is better late than never. I also believe there is a right time for everything in life. When the student is ready, the teacher will appear. If one's mind and heart is not open, there will be no acceptance and adoption even when that idea is right in front of you. And we all know that having an idea shoved down one's throat is never going to work or last. The fact that you have picked up this book might be a sign that you are open and ready to see how minimalism can transform your life. I can say that the sense of peace and freedom that comes with adopting a minimalist lifestyle is palpable and incredible! And you are the only one who needs to give yourself permission to embrace living well with less.

Becoming a minimalist is a mindset and lifestyle change. Getting rid of your clutter—physical, mental, emotional—is a result of minimalism. One needs to embrace it in both thoughts and actions, believing as well as walking the talk.

When we crave simplicity, we are not after an easier life. We are after life.

—Dave Bruno

A little word of caution

You would know by now that the road toward minimalism generally goes against the general belief and practice of conspicuous consumption and utilizing possessions as an indicator of one's creed, identity, and status. We have been programmed and brainwashed by the people around us, the media, our education, and our own past experiences that happiness is achieved through more—more money, more stuff, more friends, etc. Our status and identity is also generally determined by the house we live in, the car we drive, the job title we hold, the number of social media friends/followers we have, and so on.

So when we start to embrace "less" as a way of living more happily and fully, we might get some encouraging pats on the back, but more likely than not, we will get comments that go along the lines of: "Have you gone a little mad?" "Are you having financial difficulties?," "You can't live like a monk . . . you will not last." "Oh, does that mean we can't go shopping together anymore?" The latter is usually accompanied by some eye-rolling and worried looks. You get the drift.

In addition, I know from the experiences of many minimalists that their worst critics are those closest and dearest to them. That's probably because these people are the ones who will have to live with your new minimalist lifestyle and choices. After all this time as a minimalist, I still get some looks of incredulity from my partner. Yes, it is challenging when the people we care about have not bought into the benefits of living more with less. We can't force them to be like us, but we can show by example how living well with less is helping us to live happier and more meaningful lives. That is the best way to get others interested and engaged with minimalism.

But before we embark on the minimalism journey, let's take a look at why most of us end up with more stuff than we need.

The biggest challenge of life is to be yourself in a world that is trying to make you like everyone else.

—Anonymous

If not now, when?

Is your life on pause mode? Are you waiting for the perfect moment or that special event to happen before you get your life into full swing? When you earn X amount of money, when you meet your perfect mate, when you land yourself that dream job, etc., are you just surviving each day in anticipation of that dream day that marks the start of your perfect life? How long have you been waiting, and how much longer are you willing to wait and waste your days away before your life can truly start? You can never be a perfect person, and there is unlikely to ever be a perfect situation. What we can do is to look at what we have at the moment and build on it—one step at a time.

Just consider how this one decision to embrace minimalism will affect your entire life:

- You will recognize the false truths championed by society
- You will only own things that are of value and bring you joy
- You will identify beliefs that are holding you back
- You will recognize emotions that are impeding you
- You will spend your time with people who inspire and support you

- You will live with more purpose, intention, freedom, and intensity
- You will inspire and encourage others to live with less and gain more joy
- You will transform your life and make room for more happiness and fulfillment
- You will ultimately simplify almost every area of your life and experience a lifestyle you never thought possible

You might think now is not the time to become a minimalist; perhaps you want to sort things out before starting a new way of life. But now is always a good time to start—we can't really start living fully until we start living minimally. Minimalism gives us the opportunity to start anew.

Activity: Which of the benefits of a minimalist lifestyle listed above are you most inspired and excited by?

So what is holding you back?

Activity: Are there any reasons why you think adopting a minimalist lifestyle would be difficult or not doable for you?

If so, what are these reasons?

Is your desire for a better life great enough for you to want to find solutions around these doubts and obstacles? What are some of these solutions?

Life is what happens to us while we are making other plans.

—Allen Saunders

Chapter 2:
Stuffocation

Are we drowning in stuff?

If you were inclined to pick up this book, you probably already think that you have more stuff than you need—and that getting rid of the excess will hopefully give you more space to breathe, create, and live, as well as provide you with a sense of lightness and freedom. You are not alone. When people really start to think about it, they realize that the physical things they own are not the most important parts of their lives—they have given their stuff more meaning than they deserve.

We are evolutionarily programmed to cling onto stuff, according to James Wallman, the author of *Stuffocation*, a book on material consumption. In times of scarcity, this desire for material goods has a real survival benefit. But in the current age of abundance, this evolutionary holdover is causing us all to drown in our own glut. According to California Closets, the average person only wears around 20 percent of the clothes they own. This is particularly true among women. Most clothing goes unworn because it is the result of an impulse buy or it doesn't fit. Furthermore, the retail industry relies on these impulse purchases to stay in business! Additionally, the average woman in the UK buys fifty-nine items of clothing each year and has twice as many things in her wardrobe today as she did in 1980, including twenty-two items that she has never worn. Most of us are guilty of excess consumption in one way or another.

In a fascinating and extensive study by UCLA's Center on Everyday Lives of Families (CELF), thirty-two Los Angeles families opened their doors to CELF researchers. What they found was a staggering number of possessions and an array of spaces and furnishings that serve as the stage for multiple family activities.

The smallest home in their study was a house of 980 sq. ft. In the two bedrooms and living room alone there were 2,260 items, and those were only things the anthropologists could see when they stood still in one spot. Their rules meant they didn't count any of the stuff that was tucked into drawers or squeezed into cupboards. The other homes were just as packed. On average, each family had 39 pairs of shoes, 90 DVDs or videos, 139 toys, 212 CDs and 438 books and magazines. Nine out of ten of them had so many things that they kept household stuff in the garage. And three quarters of them had so much stuff in there that there was no room left for cars. One of the key observations researchers made was that we are living in "the most materially rich society in global history, with light-years more possessions per average family than any preceding society."

When people run out of space for their possessions at home, many will resort to renting storage facilities. The US now has 2.3 billion square feet of storage space. Fifty percent of storage renters are simply storing what wouldn't fit into their homes, even though the average size of the American home has almost doubled in the past fifty years, to 2,300 square feet. The sad thing is, most of this stuff in storage will remain unseen, unused, and forgotten.

The things you own end up owning you.

—Chuck Palahnuik

Why do we have more stuff than we need?

Most of us are likely to have more stuff than we need—that is the norm in our modern consumerist-driven society. At the individual level, the possessions we own are mistakenly perceived as being able to provide us with happiness, fulfillment, and, in some instances, comfort and security. Hence, we accumulate and consume in the hope that the more possessions we have, the happier we will become. If that was the case, why have numerous studies shown that we, as a society, are less happy now than decades ago, despite earning and owning more?

Believing that the more we have the happier we will be has generally made us unhappier and more in debt in one form or another. We all aspire to living more fully, but instead we end up with homes full of stuff, days full of mundane work, schedules full of commitments and obligations, and a life full of debt. Bigger, better, and more comes with baggage and price tags. Our expectations tend to be limitless, so satisfying them can be an endless pursuit. One of the paradoxes of modern day living is that we have too much and, at the same time, too little.

Another key driver for excessive consumption and ownership at an individual level is that we are led to believe that the things we own define who we are and how much we are worth. Our identity, status, and degree of success are commonly tied to the size of our houses, the make of the car we drive, the number of branded suits we own, etc. We are therefore programmed to signal our identity and value through the stuff we own.

We generally wear around 20 percent of the clothes and shoes we own, and we probably acquired the other 80 percent because buying them made us feel happy for a little while. These possessions helped us feel that we were "on trend" and less inadequate. But as we already know, this need to acquire things never ends; we are pressured to continue "keeping up" with perceptions and trends.

At the larger societal level, overconsumption can be the result of an unconscious act to do our bit to support the economy. Many countries continue to adopt the policy of rallying their population to spend their way out of an economic downturn. As part of that rallying call, advertising across all media constantly bombards us to buy stuff as part of an aspiration to either become someone better or purchase into a better lifestyle.

The result is more stuff than we need and more stress from working hard to buy this stuff in order to keep up appearances and maintain our lifestyle. We end up serving our stuff rather than the other way round, as it should be. Many of us spend the bulk of our life working in a job we don't like in order to buy stuff to impress people we care little for. It is no wonder that so many of us are mired in unhappiness and stress.

This book was written to offer an alternative to the "Good Life" and the "American Dream." We can live more fully with happiness and fulfillment—with less clutter and less stress. We can move on from overconsumption to curated living, where we focus on what's of value and essential to our happiness. We can shift from the "bigger is better" mentality and embrace the concept of lagom, or just enough. We can slow down our fast-paced, stressed-out lives in order to better appreciate the people and things around us. We can invest in our true passions and meaningful relationships.

There isn't anything wrong with owning stuff or with consumption. The problem arises when we give too much meaning to the stuff we own, without questioning why we own it.

Clutter costs us money (rent, storage costs) and living space; it also creates stress and mess. It is a constant annoyance and hassle (think about clearing your table space to have a meal). It makes us depressed and overwhelmed, sucking away our energy and time. To live the life that we are meant to live, we have to review our perception of consumption and relationship with clutter, both physical and otherwise.

Activity: Do you think you have more stuff than you need? Can you think of the reasons why you have accumulated all this excess stuff?

Do you think you give your possessions more meaning than they deserve?

Is your identity and worth largely defined by them?

Is this excess stuff overwhelming you and causing you stress?

Clutter is anything that stands between you
and the life you want to be living.

—Peter Walsh

Chapter 3:
The Art of Decluttering

What is a home to you?

Before we plunge into the physical act of simplifying and decluttering, I would like you to answer a couple of questions. What is a home to you, and what is it for? Is it merely a place to shelter, sleep, and wash, or is it something more? Is it a place for spending time together with loved ones, a place where you find inspiration and seek sanctuary and comfort, a place where you can be yourself?

What does your home feel like? Is it a place where there is plenty of light with sufficient space for your furnishings and belongings? Is it where you can feel relaxed and comfortable, where you can't wait to get back to after a day at work, where you would love to invite friends over to for a meal?

We are all different in what we feel makes a place a home. Apart from the common requirements, such as cleanliness and adequate space, we probably have varying needs and tastes in terms of the dream home we would want to live in.

Visualize your ideal space and lifestyle

Can you visualize your dream space and activities? Feel free to jot down the requirements, conditions, and qualities that make up your dream space. What are the furniture pieces in the space? What is the layout like? What about the color of your furnishings? What will you most enjoy doing in the space—reading, listening to your favorite music, or meditating? How will you want to feel—happy, peaceful, relaxed, and comfortable?

Why declutter?

Now look around the space you are living in. Do you enjoy the feelings that come with being here? If your answer is *no*, you have your main reason for wanting to minimalize and declutter. The ultimate aim is to be happy and peaceful in the space you inhabit.

You may ask: Is decluttering my physical stuff the most important and only way that I can feel happier, fulfilled, more peaceful, and less stressed? The answer is no. However, as you embark on your minimalist journey with this book, I will start with decluttering the physical stuff first for the following reasons.

Firstly, the physical stuff is the most obvious—it makes a visible and tangible difference when it is removed or rearranged. Hence, decluttering the physical stuff is the easiest and most motivating activity for those starting out on the minimalism journey.

Secondly, once the physical stuff is decluttered and the spaces cleared, there is a tangible feeling of freedom, peace, and relief. With the newfound physical place, we have more space to breathe, to think, and reflect. We can listen to our inner self for the optimal way to live, thrive, and feel happy and relaxed.

Activity: Collect some images (décor magazines and Pinterest are good places to start) of interior spaces that you aspire to; places that make you feel happy, calm, and comfortable. Keep these images and use them to inspire and motivate you when the decluttering gets tough.

> *Have nothing in your home that you do not know to be useful or believe to be beautiful.*
>
> —William Morris

Let the energy flow

All matter is energy. Energy is inherent in all things. In Chinese philosophy, *chi* is the name for this circulating life energy. In order for things to live, grow, and prosper, chi has to flow. Emotional blockages and physical clutter blocks the passage of chi and leads to ill health and stagnated or dead spaces, which affects both the growth and quality of your life.

The Chinese also practice the art of *feng shui*, which literally means "wind and water." The practice is to ensure that the physical placement of objects does not block the figurative flow of these two elements and their inherent energies.

The smooth and unobstructed flow of this energy is what keeps your life force alive. It opens up the space for growth to take place. Minimalism through the getting rid of the non-essentials, be it mental, emotional, or physical, is certainly pertinent and beneficial for the flow of abundant energy, which will lead to new possibilities and unlimited potential.

> *Flow is the nature of energy; the flow*
> *is another name for life.*
>
> —Banani Ray

How to declutter

Decluttering as a physical activity is rather easy and straightforward. In a nutshell, it is just asking if we should keep or discard an item. The main challenge comes from the emotions we feel when letting go. When we look at an item, we think of its physical and monetary value, the function it performs, and the information and emotional/sentimental values it holds. In order to declutter effectively, we need to ask ourselves a few key questions to break the emotional hold that our stuff has over us.

Discard first

Decluttering must first start with discarding. Decluttering without discarding is just organized hoarding. Rather than simply ask if we need or want an item, we need to ask if an item "sparks joy," as Marie Kondo advises. It makes our decluttering exercise so much easier, as well as more straightforward and effective. For example, if we have a piece of clothing that we used to wear and were hoping to wear again, the answer to "Do I need and want this?" would probably be "Yes, I'll wear it when the right occasion arrives or when I lose some weight in the future." And more often than not, we end up keeping the item. However, if we were to ask instead, "Does this item spark joy?" the answer might be different. A *yes* would mean we would keep it and a *no* would mean discarding or passing it on.

> *Don't just declutter, de-own.*
>
> —Joshua Becker

Declutter all at once

The key to successful and effective decluttering is to do it in the correct order and "all at once," preferably in a limited period of time of no more than three months. Your decluttering progress will depend on your individual motivation and circumstances, but the sooner and quicker you declutter all your belongings, the better and more significant the results will be. The aim is to make a sudden and significant transformation of the physical space, and to such an extent that it will bring about a complete change of heart and mindset. This trigger cannot be done with gradual decluttering.

When you declutter your belongings and spaces completely, you literally and figuratively transform your space—physically, mentally, and emotionally. The change in your physical surroundings is so profound that you will feel you are living in a totally new world, which in turn affects you mentally and emotionally. The state of peace, satisfaction, accomplishment, and excitement will keep you from going back to your previous cluttered state. It will also motivate you to maintain your new way of living and not lapse back into being cluttered again.

It has been a few years since I did the "big declutter" of my home, and I still remember that it took me two days and a night. Yes, I was motivated enough to want to finish the task as soon as possible, even if it meant not sleeping for a night!

Till this day, I still remember vividly that sense of freedom, lightness, and achievement of clearing out the excess; there was also the anticipation of my new life ahead. I felt I was finally free of the stuff I didn't need or want that was unconsciously weighing me down; I was finally free to create and live a life that inspired and fulfilled me.

Once you have your living space in order, you will feel your life undergo a transformation: you will have more freedom, energy, motivation, and confidence to create and live the life you want. Such a significant transformation of your living spaces can cause dramatic changes in your lifestyle as well as perspective. Remember, we are aiming for a holistic transformation of our lives on this minimalist journey.

You can turn any mess into a M.E.S.S.—Minimal, Easy to take care of, Simple to use, and Stress free.

—Kate Carpenter

Do it by category

Once we have decided to do a thorough declutter of our excess stuff in the shortest time possible, the next step is to decide where to start. It is crucial to identify how much stuff we have in each category, for example, clothing, books, and kitchenware. When we declutter, we can look at a category as a whole and determine how much we have in that category and which and how many items to keep or discard. Since many of us have items like clothing and books stored in respective rooms in our home, doing it by category will also make our task easier and more effective. We can focus on each category in turn, get a better picture of how much we have and what we really need, and avoid duplication.

When I was decluttering, I did it room by room simply because I stored each category of belongings in one place, rather than around my apartment. However, if you store different categories of stuff across various rooms, it would make more sense to declutter by category rather than by room.

In general, the main categories of our belongings are clothes, books, music and entertainment, kitchenware, bathroom toiletries, papers and information, ornaments and furnishings, and items of sentimental value. We should start with the more general items, such as clothes and kitchenware first, before moving on to more emotionally vested items like sentimental possessions and family heirlooms.

This way, we will have had enough practice in both asking ourselves the key question "Does this add value and/or have a purpose?" and making the keep/discard decisions. This will make the decluttering process more effective and efficient as we go along. Starting with more emotionally vested items will not only make the process more laborious and challenging, but it might also end up derailing the entire decluttering exercise.

To kick off the decluttering process, set yourself a time-frame and complete it as quickly as possible in order to benefit from the high that comes from the mindset change brought about by the transformation of your space.

Next, decide on the order of item categories that you will be tackling, from first to last. Ask the "value/purpose" question about every single item and make a decision whether to keep, discard, or donate. Then clean out the space before putting back the items you have decided to keep in a tidy, organized manner.

There might be items in our decluttering process that we really can't decide on. These are the "maybe/not sure" items. I would suggest that you set aside those items in a box and mark it with the date. If you have not touched those items in three months' time, it'll mean that you don't actually need or miss them. Discard these items or pass them on to others who would gain more value out of them.

Keeping things and spaces clean and organized will not only contribute to the general niceness of the space; it will also help to maintain a certain discipline in keeping it that way. Once you have experienced the loveliness and calmness of a tidy space, you will be unlikely to want to go back to living in a messy dump. With less stuff, tidying will also become a more enjoyable and efficient process. Furthermore, it is only with a tidy space that we can truly see what we have, need, and frequently use, which in turn helps to stop us from generating further clutter.

To recap, when we declutter and minimize, we must always ask:

Does this item/belief/action/relationship add any value or joy to my life?

Does it serve a purpose? If "yes," keep, if "no," discard.

Let's start off with something small.

Activity: The Wallet/Handbag Declutter

Before you embark on the "big declutter," it's useful to start off with something small in order to give yourself a little practice and evaluate how you feel after the exercise.

Your wallet, purse, or handbag are good places to start: they are things you use on a regular basis, they are typically smallish, and they also tend to accumulate a lot of junk. Most people's wallets, purses, and handbags are bloated and loaded with stuff: the useful, useless, and the "yuckies" (how about that half-eaten, melted chocolate bar?).

First, remove all the items in your wallet/purse/handbag. Go through each item and ask if it adds value and has a purpose. The really important items are probably cash, frequently used debit or credit cards, identity cards or driver's licence, and keys. Next, put the other items under the "to keep," "maybe/to store elsewhere," and "to discard" piles.

Note that we are not just looking at the value and purpose of items we have; we are also looking at the quantity. For example, many of us have a good number of cards: credit cards, membership cards, loyalty cards, etc. Evaluate if you need them all in your wallet. How important are they and how often do you use them? In a nutshell, we are not merely decluttering, we are also rationalizing our possessions to meet our true needs.

Clean your wallet/purse/handbag and the items you have decided to keep, and put the items back in an organized way.

For those of you with more than one handbag, an uncluttered and organized handbag will also help with transferring the items from one handbag to another, making sure you have everything you need when you're on the go.

Does your wallet/purse/handbag feel nicer and lighter? It should! And how do you feel? Do you feel better and "lighter," too?

Another easy decluttering exercise to help us get started is to clean out any junk (for example, junk mail or things that are broken or of no use) and multiples of items (for example, the big stash of pens we have in the drawer).

Ready for the main declutter?
Let's start!

Clothes. Many of us have more clothes than we need. The general consensus is that we tend to regularly wear only about 30 percent of what we own. We own clothes that we don't wear for a number of reasons, including impulse purchases, sales bargains (remember: if you don't buy clothes on 50 percent sales, you save 100 percent!), keeping up with what's in fashion, or because they no longer fit us. We should match our clothing needs with our lifestyle and preferences, rather than by what fashion dictates we should be wearing. We look best in clothes that we feel good and comfortable in.

We might be tempted to keep certain clothes in case we are able to fit into them one day when we lose that few extra pounds or for a special occasion. But as we all know, that one day seldom comes along. So, live for today and wear what is right for you now. When that one day finally arrives, reward yourself by buying a pair of jeans that is two sizes smaller or a lovely black dress that will make that special occasion even more special.

When I decluttered my wardrobe, I was no longer working in a corporate job, but I loathed discarding all those suits and kept thinking I would put them into service again when I went back to work. But then I thought, *I am unlikely to want to work in an environment again that requires suits; and even if I did, I would buy new suits. In the meantime, these suits would be better served going to others who would get more value out of them.* They went to the charity shop pile.

When it comes to clothes, my ethos is to embrace less but better, and quality over quantity. It is worthwhile owning a wardrobe of clothes we love and wear frequently, and every piece of clothing should be our favorite piece. We should also invest in quality clothing that is well made and looks good, regardless of the trends of the day.

It is a conscious choice to buy clothing that might cost a bit more but that is of a higher quality and will not come apart after a few wears. Additionally, such clothing has not been made by people who are paid a pittance for their work. Consequently, we end up with a well-curated wardrobe that takes up less space; it'll also take up less of our time, especially during the moments when we decide what we should be wearing that day. It is worth remembering that the bitterness of poor quality remains long after the sweetness of the low price is forgotten.

Books. I love books. Being an avid reader, frequent bookshop browser, and former books business owner, I had hundreds of books and still own quite a number after my big declutter. From my own experience and those of others, especially the book lovers I have spoken to, decluttering books is one of the biggest challenges in the whole decluttering exercise.

Books pile up because we acquire them at a faster rate than we are able to read them. And once we have read a book, we tend to keep them if we enjoyed it or in case we want to read it again. But how often do we reread books? In most cases, only a few favorite titles are worth keeping. A significant number of my books went onto the charity pile once I realized I was unlikely to ever have the time or the inclination to reread them, especially when I still have so many new titles to read.

It is a little more difficult when you own unread books. We tell ourselves we'll read them sometime in the future, but the truth is that many of those volumes will never get read (at least in my personal experience). There are always new books to be bought, and our interest tends to move on with new acquisitions. The best approach to this is to read the books the moment you purchase them!

When it comes to books, keep only those you really love and will reread. Be honest with yourself. Keep these to a minimum and donate or discard the rest. To keep your book collection from getting out of hand again, consider using the library and only purchasing books that you will read in the near future.

An electronic book reader will also help to keep the physical books in check. I tend to buy eBook versions of novels that I know I'll read once and never again, nonfiction books that I love and want to have with me on my Kindle, and travel guides and reference books, which are good to have on hand so I can access them easily. Reference books and travel guides tend to be especially bulky, while e-book versions allow easier accessibility and portability—and they also benefit from content updates.

Like the rest of your belongings, a decluttered book collection will give you a great sense of joy and lightness. What's left on the bookshelf will be your favorite books that you look forward to reading sometime soon!

Music and entertainment. Music and entertainment items are very similar to books and they can build up quite easily and quickly. Unlike books, we tend to listen to musical pieces over and over again. When decluttering our music collection, we should only keep the music we love and still listen to. It is the same for the films we own.

Just like clothes, we might have purchased music that used to be at the top of the charts but that we have since outgrown. These should go into the discard or donate pile. Advances in technology also mean we no longer need to own physical CDs or records to listen to our favorite tracks as they can now be streamed or downloaded, saving us space in the process. Various movie and TV services such as Netflix also mean that we no longer need to hold on to a library of discs in order to watch shows we enjoy whenever we want.

Kitchenware. The amount of kitchenware should align with your needs and the size of your household. Is there a need to get six of every cutlery and crockery item when there are only two of you? Also, do you use the kitchen appliances you own on a regular basis? Is there a need for that bread maker when you only use it twice a year? The kitchen is also a hotspot for duplicates—do you actually need two cheese graters?

Toiletries. This category is generally easier for men to tackle rather than women, mainly because most women have a lot more toiletries and make-up. The key here is once again to look at our regular cleansing and beauty routine, and focus on the items we use most frequently. Organize these items neatly, and discard items that we no longer use or that have expired.

I used to get stressed about packing my toiletries whenever I traveled. After my big declutter, they all now fit into a small toiletries bag. I use this bag at home and simply take the whole bag with me when I travel. It has saved a lot of stress and packing time!

Paperwork. Papers of all types can contribute a lot to mess and clutter. Even if they are properly filed and organized, they can still take up quite a bit of physical space. There are generally three types of paperwork: important documents, such as birth and marriage certificates, passports, and educational qualifications; warranties and user manuals; and bills and other reference/notepapers.

It is best to put all important documents in one place so that they can be accessed easily. I put all my important documents in a bag, so I can grab the bag if I need them or if there is an emergency. I also have scanned copies of these documents so that they can be accessed across my devices and online.

All warranties and user manuals should also be stored together in a file. Once a year or so, warranties should be reviewed and the expired ones discarded. Personally, I find user manuals to be a waste of space as most of us can probably use our new equipment quite well without referring to manuals.

I discard all of my user manuals now. Most manufacturers also provide online manuals and user forums, so there is little reason to keep these bulky papers. The same goes for catalogs. Many companies provide online catalogs that can be browsed without cluttering up space.

Much of our paper clutter is probably bills, notes, and other reference papers. I have opted for online billing as much as possible as it cuts down on the clutter and the amount of mail you receive. If you still have paper bills, they should be stored in a "for action" file, along with other paperwork that requires action in one form or another. Once actioned, the bills and paperwork can be discarded. As for other reference and notepapers, scanning them is a good way to reduce the space they take up.

Photos. There is a sentimental value as memories and experiences are embedded in photos. That's why we take them and keep them, and also why they are quite hard to part with. Before you know it, photos fill up entire albums and take up space in multiple storage boxes. I used to have eight albums filled with photos of one of my trips to Italy. Okay, it was an extended stay of a couple of months, but eight albums? When I was decluttering and looked through these albums, I could barely remember half the names of the places where the photos were taken.

With digital photography, we can now "click" with abandon, as each image will cost us nothing in film and processing costs. However, even though they don't take up physical space, they fill up memory space.

When I started decluttering my photos, I bought a 250-photo album. All the ones I decided to keep would have to fit into that album alone. It was a challenge, but I managed it. The key photos, from my birth until now, are all stored in that single album—a curated selection of my most memorable and beautiful moments and my milestones, as well as the people and vistas from my travels. I have since gone a step further by scanning these photos and storing them on my phone and laptop for easy access and backup.

I have also applied the same principle of "less but better" to my postcards. I used to load up on postcards of places I had traveled to, on top of all the photos I'd taken. Have I ever looked at those postcards again? No. Hundreds of these postcards were discarded or donated to charity shops. I only kept a few that I really liked. I have since refrained from buying postcards, and if I do, they are of scenes I can't take with my camera.

As with paperwork, a scanner can be your best friend when it comes to storing photos. Effective storage is one thing, but the best way to avoid an overload of photos is to be mindful of what and how many we take. We have all probably been here: we end up standing in front of a beautiful place and going *click, click, click.*

As part of my minimalist journey, I have become more mindful. When I see beautiful scenery in front of me now, I take the time to first admire the beauty and soak up the atmosphere, so that I fully live and appreciate the moment and experience in front of me. Only then will I get my camera out and take a few shots. One doesn't need ten shots of the Eiffel Tower. A few well-taken images will convey the scene and mood just as well, if not better. Once again, for photos, the concept is "less but better."

Sentimental items. Items that have been bequeathed to us by loved ones, letters from an old romantic relationship, our children's report cards and artwork, and other possessions imbued with family ties and deep memories are not easy to discard or pass on. We keep and maybe treasure these items because they remind us of loved ones and strong experiences. But how many of these items do we truly love and treasure, and how many do we keep out of a sense of duty?

We may cling to these items because we think they represent our loved ones who are no longer with us, or the love, pleasures, and memories that the people related to these items have brought us. But this way of thinking is mostly mistaken. Yes, the items may serve as reminders of strong memories and emotions, but these memories and emotions within us, independent of these physical objects, will continue to exist.

I am certainly not saying that we are free to discard or pass on all of these possessions. Well, yes, you can discard some if you want to, but most of us would probably want to retain a number of these items. The questions to ask, then, are: Do we love them? Do they add value or serve a purpose? Do we need all of them?

Also, we might need to apply some form of curation here. Do we need to keep Aunt Edith's entire dining service when there are only two members in the household? Instead of keeping your child's entire artwork collection, pick a few good, representative ones that you really like. Find spaces to display the items you love and chose to keep. Before discarding or donating the rest, take a photo of them to retain as a keepsake.

This list of what items to declutter is certainly not exhaustive; you probably have more stuff in your home that has not been listed here. But the principle is always the same: Does it add value or serve a purpose? Does it spark joy? If yes, keep it. If not, discard or pass it on.

At this point, you might ask, "How much decluttering do I need to do? How do I know when it is done?" The answers to these questions will vary from individual to individual.

Remember, minimalism is a very personal journey, and there is no strict rule that outlines when you have too little or too much. Instead, there is a "just right" for everyone, which varies from one person to another. Speaking from personal experience, you will know instinctively when you have done enough—when the items you've chosen to keep and the spaces you have freed up are just right for you at that moment in your life. Needless to say, what sparks joy or adds value today might not do so in the future, so it is always useful to review your belongings on a regular basis.

Here are some key tips to help you with your decluttering:

* Declutter to lagom—just the right amount for your needs
* Create some clear space for the chi to flow and calmness to prevail
* You need a place for everything, and everything needs its place
* Take pictures of sentimental things you have chosen to discard. You can still have the memories that don't take up space!
* Ask yourself the questions: "If I had to start my life from scratch, what would I need?" "If I only had a suitcase to fill, what are the things I would put in it?" This will help us to focus on what is really essential.

Don't forget the virtual stuff

In the previous section, we covered how we can declutter the physical stuff around us, leaving us with only items that add value or serve a purpose in our lives and freeing up the physical space and reducing time, effort, and stress of ownership and maintenance in the process. However, some of the stuff that takes up mental and emotional space is not physical but virtual. These include email, social media, computer files, and digital books and music.

The same principle of "adding value and serving a purpose" applies to virtual stuff. Just like its physical counterpart, virtual stuff can take up memory space in the Cloud. Its presence does require our investment in one way or another, as too much of it will invariably cause stress, confusion, and distraction. Decluttering and organizing virtual stuff will enable us to focus on what's really important, adding joy and value and freeing up some space in the process!

Email. Many of us have suffered from an overflowing email inbox at one time or another, and maybe still do. An inbox filled with unread and unanswered emails is a source of stress. It makes us feel out of control. Sometimes, we even give up sorting out the mail due to a sense of overwhelm. Having an empty or small inbox is similar to having a clean and clear desk; we feel in control and calm, and we have the space to focus on our task at hand.

If your inbox is out of control, there are two ways you can rein it back in. The first is to delete all of the emails in your inbox and start again. Yes, that's right. Select all mail and press "delete." Voila! Your slate is clean and you can begin from scratch. It takes a brave soul to do that. One might say, "What if there is an important email in there?" or "What if I'm deleting a to-do list? I won't know what to do next without it." Well, if the email was that important, shouldn't it be filed somewhere or acted on instead of being hidden among the hundreds of other emails?

I remember returning to work once after a holiday to find my inbox chockablock with emails. There was a double accumulation of emails as they included unsorted messages that had been sent to me before I left and emails that had arrived while I was on holiday. This left me feeling very stressed, overwhelmed, and certainly not in control, and I was frozen into inaction because I simply did not know where to begin. After a strong cup of coffee (that always helps!), I decided that I was going to begin anew. I pressed "select all" in my inbox, followed by "delete." *Whoosh.* Hundreds of emails were gone! The sense of freedom was quite exhilarating! I told myself that if I had happened to delete anything important, I would know soon enough or be told or reminded about it. After two days, there was no catastrophe. I was not fired for clearing my inbox and my colleagues kindly re-sent me the few emails that needed to be reviewed or approved.

The second and probably more digestible method of clearing an inbox is to knuckle down and sort out your emails one by one. As you go through each email, decide if it needs to be actioned, if it is for future reference, if it is for specific projects, or if it should be trashed. There will be some emails that can be responded to immediately and then trashed. The rest can be filed under the "action" or "for reference" folders. Just make sure you go through and action the emails in the "action" folder regularly or they can overflow and get out of control.

Constantly checking emails can be a huge distraction and waste of time, diverting our focus away from the key tasks at hand. The most optimal method for managing emails is to set aside one or two periods during the day (about 15–30 minutes each time) just for reading, responding, processing, and filing emails, and clearing out the inbox. It might also help to notify others of your email response times so they do not expect an email from you straight away. It requires a certain level of discipline and diligence, but once it becomes a habit, we will always have a "zen inbox."

Social media. Can anyone remember what our life was like before Facebook, Twitter, et al., came along? What were we doing to fill the time when there was a lull in conversation?

What did we do when we were waiting for our meals to arrive, waiting for the train, traveling on public transport, and generally feeling bored? For the most part, social media has been very beneficial for our social connections and has kept us up to date with the world around us. But for many, myself included, we have at some time or other fallen victim to mindless scrolling of timeline statuses and feeds, and some of our connections and communications with "friends" have been reduced to liking and retweeting.

We need to rationalize our social media usage not just for the sake of minimizing, but also because reviewing our usage adds value—ensuring they are not just mindless time fillers or a substitute for real face-to-face connections.

Personally, I make a point to accept friend requests only from people I am actually friends with, and I have even tried to keep it to a certain number (sixty is the current threshold). To me, my social media connections are not about reaching a number that indicates my social connection kudos, where the more "friends" I have, the better I am rated. Instead, I have chosen to use it as one of the platforms I use to connect with my real friends. Here, it is about quality over quantity. The same principle applies to page likes and the people and groups I follow.

Secondly, I try to limit the number of times and time duration I look at my social media platforms and other online sites. I lose focus if I check my social media sites or surf websites too frequently. They end up being mindless distractions that turn me away from my task at hand with no conscious connections or benefit, just like surfing TV channels.

There is no right amount of time to spend online; it varies from individual to individual. One way to tell if you are just mindlessly surfing is to gauge how you feel afterwards. If I have been surfing mindlessly, I feel a bit guilty about the time I have wasted and deflated because I have not gained anything valuable from my activity. On the other hand, if I manage to stick to my limits on online usage and the browsing is a lot more conscious and deliberate, I tend to feel as if I have gained something out of the session—be it interaction, information, or entertainment.

It can also help to take some time off from being online. These offline times could last a day, a week, or after working hours. Or you might decide not to go online during meals or for specific periods, such as an hour before you go to bed.

I know quite a number of people who do not have, or who have cancelled, their social media accounts because they think social media is superficial and does not add value, or, they simply want to free their time up for more constructive activities. For the rest of us, social media and online activities might serve a purpose; however, the aim is to ensure that we consciously control our online activities rather then browse mindlessly and use it as a form of distraction or a cure for boredom. This will free up our time so we can use it on activities that we enjoy and that add value, such as having a phone conversation or coffee with friends instead of just reading about each other's life updates on Facebook.

Computer files and phone apps. I have seen the home screens of many phones and laptops that are full of applications, files, and documents. I don't know about you, but this raises my stress levels and is a reflection of disorganized chaos. An uncluttered or clear home screen is similar to a cleared desk, providing calm, order, and a distraction-free space. My phone and laptop screens used to be cluttered with apps, documents, and files, which contributed to my chaos. Furthermore, the apps and files I wanted at a given moment in time were always difficult to find in the mess. I couldn't even see, let alone enjoy, the beautiful picture of the Rocky Mountains in Colorado I used as a wallpaper.

Inspired by Leo Babauta of the *Zen Habits* blog, I cleared all the files and documents from my laptop screen and filed them neatly into relevant document files and folders in my File Manager. I have also minimized the applications icons that I use frequently to the icon bar at the bottom of my screen. Now I see the breathtaking view of the mountains whenever I look at my home screen—priceless! I have also decluttered and organized the apps on my phone so that only the ones I use frequently appear—saving me both access time and memory space.

Digital books/music/videos. Many do not consider digital material to be clutter, mainly because it is housed in electronic devices and doesn't take up physical space. However, if clutter is anything that does not add value or serve a purpose, then digital books, music, and videos we have already consumed or will not use again serve little purpose except to take up memory space. We should review our digital material once in a while and go through what we want to keep or delete, in order to create more space for new content we truly enjoy.

How do you feel about decluttering after having read the above paragraphs? Are you pumped up? Can't wait to fill up the trash bags with excess stuff? Or are you feeling overwhelmed and simply don't know where to begin? Here's an activity to help you get started.

Activity: Start small, start somewhere, start a habit.

Start your decluttering with a small project (for example, your wallet or a drawer) and a small space (for example, your desk or the kitchen countertop).

Start somewhere. It doesn't matter what or where you start decluttering, but start somewhere.

Start a habit of doing something on a regular basis. It can be just 5 minutes of clearing out each day before dinner or a dedicated weekend to clear the garage. But make it a regular habit, and do something (decluttering, tidying, cleaning), no matter how little, on a regular basis. Every little bit helps toward progress, and it's a small but concrete step toward a new way of living.

You don't need more space, you need less stuff.

—Anonymous

Keeping it up

Now that you have decluttered your physical and virtual spaces, how can you continue to keep this up? Ideally, decluttering and tidying should not be done daily, but rather as a special one-off event. It should just be maintenance afterward and a case of simply storing things where they belong. The goal is to establish the lifestyle that you want once your home is in order. Decluttering is just a tool and not the destination. Here are a few more pointers to keep you on track and clutter-free.

Lagom. We mentioned this Swedish word at the beginning of the book, and I'd like to elaborate on it a bit more, not only because it is one of my favorite minimalism concepts, but also because it basically underpins what minimalism and simple living entails. Lagom, or "exactly the right amount" or "enough," allows for more than enough, but still sets limits. It is about what one actually needs, which can vary from person to person, rather than about what one wants; and it points to joy rather than deprivation. I own one set of bed sheets and four bath towels. I change and wash my bed sheets and put them on again after they are dry. I only need two towels—one to use, while the other is in the wash. The other two towels are for guests. This linen setup is just right for my needs and saves me much hassle and storage space. More than "enough" is excess baggage.

Self-image and self-worth. Consuming can make us feel good or more worthy and so starve off feelings of inadequacy for a while. However, it is a never-ending pursuit. The novelty will wear off, and there will always be that next branded handbag or new car model to make us feel even more attractive or successful. The way to break the pattern is to understand that you are good, lovely, and worthy as you are without these external objects. No one is judging you as a person by the dress you are wearing or the house you own. If they are, it might be worth evaluating if they are people you want to spend your time with.

Security and "just in case." We tend to accumulate stuff because, at some level, they help us to feel safe and protected, shielding us from the effects of an emotional, natural, or economic disaster. However, more often than not, our worst fears do not materialize, and we are left holding on to all the extra stuff. I am not referring to keeping the pantry well stocked or that extra torchlight for emergencies. Try asking yourself these questions: What is the worst-case scenario that can happen?

Can you do without these items? Who can you rely on? What can you live without? In many cases, we purchase and hold on to stuff for these just-in-case scenarios. Personally, the only just-in-case item I own is my medicine and first aid pouch.

Comfort. When we are feeling depressed, stressed, or lonely, we tend to seek comfort in mindless consumption of new material stuff, food, and entertainment. These avenues provide comfort because, rather than judge us, they act as a security blanket. However, they are temporary and will not help to solve your problems. Instead, they will possibly make things worse with more clutter, more debt, and more health issues. The way to deal with problems is not through escape but by looking them straight in the eye, acknowledging them, and dealing with them in a manageable and constructive way.

Memories and living in the past. Photos, souvenirs, old correspondence, etc., hold many emotions and memories of the past—of good times and the people we care about. The past is important, but while it was once part of our lives, it isn't anymore. We don't need these items to represent the people we love or those special moments. What's truly important and memorable will always live inside us.

Similarly, items given to us by those we love, such as birthday cards from our family or a gift from our partner, do not fully manifest their feelings for us. Realize that things are not love, only representations of it. It would be more rewarding to express and receive love by being with that person and spending time together with them.

By all means, keep some selected photos and mementos of special people and important events and enjoy them. But we will stay stuck in the past if we keep everything, and it will stop us from both living more fully in the present and looking forward into the future. Do not live your life by looking at the rearview mirror; rather, it is ahead of you.

Possibilities and living in the future. We can buy and hold on to stuff with the aim of using it sometime in the future. These could be Spanish books you bought to learn the language or the new bread maker you purchased to make your own bread. More often than not, that "sometime" never arrives, and these items end up unused and clutter up the space. That's how that person you know ends up with a beautiful tea service that has been saved up for that rare special occasion. But it makes me wonder if they are ever going to enjoy the tea set, especially when they are already in their eighties! Do what you are happy and excited about now, for there is always a right moment for everything. Own things that you love or that you can use now, and not for some possibility in the future. Make a decision to keep items for up to three months—if you have not used them by then, discard or pass them on to someone who will find them more relevant and useful.

I used to buy and accumulate things for that special occasion or for when I planned to buy my dream home. But then I realized I was holding back my life and living for the future. Life's too short and precious for that. If it's a choice to live in the past, present, or future, we should always choose to live in the now.

Duplicates. Much of our clutter can be attributed to duplicate items. How many pens do you have scattered around your spaces? Do you need that many? Do you know that you have three cheese graters in the kitchen that are exactly the same? We acquire items for just-in-case scenarios, and, more often than not, we do not even know if we already own one or multiple copies of the item, as they are buried in all the stuff and mess around us (hence, the importance of tidying and keeping things in their right places)! Start to rationalize the quantity of similar items that you have, and then see what a difference it makes to have more space and less clutter.

The price of stuff. We are inspired to purchase stuff that is on sale, including things we don't need or even particularly like, in order not to miss out on a deal. We might save 50 percent on the sale, but if we didn't buy stuff we didn't need, we would actually end up saving 100 percent of our money. On the other hand, we also tend to be reluctant to dispose of or donate items that we don't really need anymore because we remember the amount of money we originally paid for them—this is known as sunk costs. If that's the case, ask yourself if you would be willing to pay the same amount of money for that item today. If the answer is yes, keep it because it means enough to you that you would want to pay for it again. If the answer is no, this means that you don't really care for it, so discard it or pass it on to others who might want it more. There is no point hanging on to an item just because you have invested time and money in it in the past but it doesn't add any value to your current life.

It is not about organizing. You might be tempted to think that you will create more space and get rid of the clutter and mess by buying storage boxes, or even renting storage space and putting everything neatly in their appointed space. However, and I hate to say this, you will then just be rearranging the clutter. You must always discard first before storing—or storage could easily end up as organized hoarding!

It is up to you if you want it to be a numbers game. Some people decide that they only want to own a certain number of items. It could be a hundred items in total (Dave Bruno's "The 100 Thing Challenge"), thirty-three items over three months of clothing (Courtney Carver of Be More With Less and her Project 333) or fifty books and no more. Others choose to practice the "one in one out" system, whereby they would get rid of one item before they purchase another, in order to keep their amount of belongings constant and manageable.

Personally, I don't practice the numbers, not because I don't think they are good systems to follow, but because I like to keep things organic. My needs and taste evolve over time, and I have enough faith in myself to know what I need and when I have enough. I don't want to be restricted by mere numbers. However, as mentioned before, minimalism is tailored to each individual's needs. For some, keeping an eye on the number of items they own might work very well.

Keep your essentials in one bag. I always have five things with me when I am out and about: my wallet, keys, phone, driver's license, and passport. I also keep all my important documents and mementos in one small carry bag next to my bedside table. It gives me peace of mind to know exactly where my important stuff is. If there is a grab-and-run emergency, I'll just grab that bag and go.

Invest in joy and beauty. In the process of simplifying and decluttering, we must not neglect the importance of beauty, which can provide much joy. For example, we might have decluttered our big mug collection down to four pieces. These mugs might be functional, but do you find them beautiful and a pleasure to use?

After embarking on my minimalist journey and after my big declutter, I actually spent a few thousand dollars buying stuff. Yes, you read that correctly: I went on a shopping spree! You see, during this transformative process, I got a much deeper understanding of what makes me happy and what meets my needs and aesthetic tastes. For example, pre-minimalism, I was into Balinese décor, and a number of my furniture pieces were dark and bulky in an attempt to evoke the feeling of living a carefree island life in a Victorian flat in London. This dark furniture no longer gives me joy, instead they feel rather oppressive. So I sold or donated the furniture that no longer gave me pleasure and replaced them with items that I found aesthetically pleasing and that met my new needs and taste.

Sometimes, simplifying your life also requires the purchase of more stuff. A good example is my mini iPad, which I use for computing and internet browsing, and also as my e-book reader. It has allowed me to cut down and rationalize the number of physical books I own. So do not be afraid of investing in things that give you joy and that add value and beauty into your life. Remember, minimalism is a joy, not a deprivation.

Appreciate the empty spaces. As we rid ourselves of excess stuff, we will end up with more space: empty spaces and even empty rooms. Many of us might be tempted to fill these newly emptied spaces with more stuff, but give it some deep consideration before doing so. Learn to appreciate these spaces and the calm and freedom they bring. With less stuff, you now have more space than you need, and this might give you a reason to consider lowering your financial burden through downsizing your home.

Focus on experiences. Instead of buying things as a way to find happiness and identity, consider experiences instead. Apart from having less clutter, you would probably derive more satisfaction from your experiences. Memories live longer than physical things. Unlike things, memories cannot be taken away from you. Choose to spend quality time with your loved ones, cook a meal together, enjoy a conversation, watch your favorite movie, visit an exhibition, or embark on that road trip you've always dreamed about—the list is endless. After all, experiences are like life—they are meant to be lived and relived. Also, isn't it more fun to have stories to tell rather than stuff to show?

Procrastination. Sometimes, we know that the stuff around us is not necessary; they cause us stress and do not add value to our lives. Yet we continue to live with this clutter because we find it too difficult to deal with. Clutter is procrastination! Similar to other mental and emotional issues, we live with clutter, hoping that it'll go away or that we'll learn to tolerate and accept it. But by putting it off or putting up with it, things will only get worse, and the stress of delaying builds up inside us, impeding us from moving on and affecting the quality of our lives.

Take it one step at a time, but start somewhere. Take one piece and deal with that. Start feeling good, then take on the next step. Sometimes we need the help and support of others, so don't be afraid to ask. We make more progress if we are accountable to others and have fun in the process.

Mindset change. As you go through the reviewing and decluttering process, your mindset and behavior toward consumption and possession also tends to evolve and change. You will be more mindful of the need for an item before purchasing it and more conscious of whether a belonging is worth keeping or if it's time to let it go.

After my big declutter, I took a weekday off (I would not be able to cope with such as an exercise on a weekend!) and headed off to the biggest mall in west London. In my pre-minimalist days, I would have had to buy something—anything—even if it was a newspaper to make me feel the outing had been worthwhile. As I browsed and walked past the rows upon rows of shops, I stopped occasionally to take a closer look, but there was no desire to buy. At that moment, I realized I had all I needed and I didn't need anything else. Minimalism is not anti-consumption; I see it as conscious, mindful consumption and ownership.

Identify the essential. Eliminate the rest.

—Leo Babauta

Chapter 4:
Empowerment through Self-Knowledge, Focus, and Intention

Let your true self show

Adopting a minimalist lifestyle does not only transform our physical space as described in the previous chapters. The transformation of our physical environment also brings about psychological and emotional changes; they are all part of a holistic mindset and lifestyle shift.

So, let's now turn the focus on us. We are all unique and special in our own ways. There is no one in this world that is exactly like us, even if we have an identical twin. However, many of us choose to hide, repress, and even fake who we really are so that we can be one of the masses and not stand out like a sore thumb. We try to conform to the mainstream and do what's expected of us in order to avoid being the odd one out. As social beings, the thought of being on one's own—an outcast—and not part of the "in crowd" is quite frightening.

The fear of being our true selves with all its faults, warts, and shortcomings and the potential to be subjected to disapproval and criticism amounts to us giving away the power to make ourselves happy. And that is even more frightening!

Much of this fear boils down to a lack of confidence in ourselves to be truly who we are. We hide behind a facade and repress our authenticity because of our ego—that mental eye from which we see ourselves in relation to other people. We lack the self-esteem to believe that we can survive and thrive without the constant approval and support of those around us.

The least we can do to make our limited time in this world worthy and well lived is to have the courage to live a life that is true to our values and dreams, instead of living the life people expect of us. We should not be measured by definitions and benchmarks that are laid out by others.

Follow your dreams and pursue what makes you happy. Take control of your life and identify what gives you joy. This will create a well-lived life. Wear the clothes you love and are comfortable in, rather than those you are expected to wear. Quit the job you loathe to travel the world, if that's what you've always wanted to do; open up that café you've always been dreaming of; or downsize to a smaller house that suits your needs and finances better. We only live but once, so embrace your authentic self and lead the life you were meant to live. Be free. At the end of the day, you are the only one you have to be accountable to.

Activity: Set aside a quiet moment and review how authentically you are living your life. Do you spend the bulk of your time being who you truly are, doing what you're passionate about, and being open and honest with people around you? If yes, great! If not, list the situations where you are hiding behind a façade and ask the reasons why.

What is the worst that can happen if you come out from behind these walls and start living more in line with your true self? Would you be more happy and fulfilled?

Acknowledgment of where you are in relation to being your true self and living the life you're meant to live is a good first step toward self-knowledge and actualization.

Your time is limited, so don't waste it on living someone else's life.

—Steve Jobs

Live by your own expectations

In the previous section, we talked about living authentically. The practice of living by your own expectations is very much part of that authenticity.

We have probably already experienced living by our own expectations and by those of others. Our parents and teachers have certain expectations of our behaviors, grades, and future careers; our friends have expectations of how they would like us to act for clique identity; and we have expectations to not fail ourselves and those around us. At the end of the day, you know best in terms of what gives you joy, fulfillment, and the room to breathe. Always ask yourself first who you can be, what you can do, and what makes it work for you.

Definition of success

Success is something that only you can define and achieve for yourself. The opinions of others are not essential. So what if the rest of the world says that the definition of success is a minimum of a one-hundred-thousand-dollar yearly salary, a nice house in an upper class district, a German luxury car, and so on? If it gives you joy and fulfillment to pursue those success markers, then by all means aim for them. However, most of us yearn for something else deep down.

We find out soon enough that the above hallmarks of success come at a price: a sense of emptiness that refuses to go away in spite of the achievements. There is in turn little time for our loved ones; our health suffers from the workload and pressure; and if we are being totally honest, we are not truly happy. How is this a "success" if it doesn't give us joy and fulfillment? So define your own success, be it having a loving family, being a good partner or parent, owning your own successful business, working for your dream company, or traveling the world for a year. If it delivers joy and purpose to you, that's success.

Activity: What defines success for you currently? Are these benchmarks defined by others, or are they what is right for you? Can you revise your success benchmarks to align them with your own beliefs, values, and passions?

Being and doing enough

It is important to both know when we have enough and also when we are being and doing enough. There is always going to be more to be, more to do, and more to have. The expectations of others might impel us to reach way beyond our limits, resulting in our own suffering and failure. It is up to us to set our own limits, ones that are reasonable, reachable, and gratifying, leaving us the space to relax and enjoy life. As Greg McKeown, author of *Essentialism*, said: "If you don't prioritize your life, someone else will."

Learn to say no

So, how do we set aside the space and resources that are just enough for our happiness? For many of us, saying yes is easy; saying no is usually not. We don't want to disappoint, reject, be socially awkward, or miss out on a potential opportunity. If we have difficulty saying no to more consumption, more work, more activities, more commitments, and a full schedule, sooner or later we will find ourselves overwhelmed and burned out. We should know what our priorities are. And given the twenty-four hours in a day, the fulfillment of these priorities should come first. Instead, we should say yes to the people and activities that give us joy and fulfillment. We should say yes to the things and activities we enjoy, not because we are obliged to do so. And we should say no to the rest.

Many of us fear missing out on things (FOMO), but we need to realize that there is also joy in missing out (JOMO).

It is only when we permit ourselves to stop trying to do it all and stop saying yes to everyone that we are able to make our highest contribution toward the people and things that really matter.

> *Ask yourself what is really important and then have the courage to build yourself around your answer.*
>
> —Anonymous

Stop the glorification of being busy

We live in a busy world where our worth and importance are often measured in terms of our productivity, efficiency, and how tight our schedules are. We are inundated with commitments, appointments, status updates, and meetings as we all try to cram as much as possible into twenty-four hours. Busy has become the new norm. If you are not busy, you are often thought of as lazy, unproductive, inefficient, unimportant, and a waste of space.

Back when I was working in the corporate world, I felt the pressure to fill up my schedule with meetings, look busy while at my desk, and walk briskly from one place to another to keep up the appearance of needing to be somewhere at all times. It seems comical now, but I am sure that, at one time or another, we have all been busy trying to look busy.

There is nothing wrong with being busy (or not busy)— the question is what are we busy with? Busy for the sake of being busy (or looking busy) is like spending precious energy and resources on various tasks aimed at different directions, hoping that some of it will work and produce a satisfactory outcome. We need to ask ourselves the reason for and purpose of doing something, and whether it adds any value or contributes toward any progress. Working hard and cramming our schedules may not necessarily deliver better results. In fact, it might even have the opposite effect. Also, rushing around and overworking is likely to have a negative impact on our general well-being as we'll be left with little time to rest and recuperate or to reflect and truly appreciate the task at hand. Stress and burnout are the likely results of such a high-octane lifestyle.

So take time to slow down. Reclaim control of your time and your life. Appreciate the meal you are eating, the conversation you are having, or the project you are working on. Focus on being there and not rushing mindlessly toward its completion in order to start the next thing. As Carl Honoré said in his book *In Praise of Slowness*, being slow means you control the rhythms of your own life. "You decide how fast you have to go in any given context. If today I want to go fast, I will go fast; if tomorrow I want to go slow, I go slow. What we are fighting for is the right to determine our own tempos."

Activity: Review your commitments and appointments for the day, week, and month ahead. Are they adding value to your life, or are they simply in your calendar because of obligation and the expectations of others?

Start crossing out the commitments and activities that do not add value and reclaim more time and space for yourself and things that matter.

It is not enough to be busy. The question is what are we busy about?

—Henry David Thoreau

Finding focus in a world of distraction

In the previous section, we looked at why it is not good enough to be busy for the sake of being busy. We need to ask ourselves: what are we busy with? What value and purpose does it serve in the end, apart from giving us stress and burnout? Instead of trying to be busy, we should aim to be focused. If we can focus on one task at a time, we will be much more effective, and our energy will be channeled into the task at hand in the most efficient manner.

There are discernible differences between being busy and being focused. Being busy involves movement and motion with the aim of just "ticking the boxes" and "getting things done." It works well for mundane, repetitive, and uniform work, but it's not so great for work that requires awareness, intention, thought, ideation, evaluation, creation, and appreciation. By being focused, one might not get as much accomplished as by being busy. But the end result will be more intentional and significant.

You might say, "I am great at multitasking; I see no problem in doing more than one thing at a time and getting them done." I, too, was once a great believer in my multitasking prowess. In an age where busyness and doing more in less time is valued, multitasking has become a must-have skill to include on nearly every CV that is going to have the slightest chance of being looked at. However, most recently multitasking, once thought to be a positive skill, has been proven to decrease concentration and productivity. It is simply cognitive overload.

The myth of multitasking being useful and efficient has been debunked with the reality that when you spread your attention and effort across various tasks, you are only giving 50 percent or less to each task. This means that the result and output will be less than optimum and satisfactory. As Seneca said, "To be everywhere is to be nowhere."

The 80/20 rule

If we have limited time and a whole list of things to do, what is the best way of getting the optimum result while also staying focused? This is where the 80/20 rule or Pareto rule might come in useful. The 80/20 rule is the observation that about 20 percent of your effort brings about 80 percent of your results, or that 80 percent of the effects come from 20 percent of the causes. Sometimes, what we don't do is just as important as what we do. So focus on those 20 percent of ideas, beliefs, relationships, activities, and commitments that deliver 80 percent of your joy, value, results, and achievement.

Blocking out time

Another great way to break free from the multitasking habit and stay focused is to block out your workday into small chunks of time and then work uninterrupted for that period on a specific task. I find that my productivity and progress slows down significantly when I interspace working on my task with checking messages, emails, browsing the web and social media, or even going to make a cup of coffee. Block out separate times for these other activities and try to focus and get rid of other distractions. You will find that you will be able to achieve much more in terms of productivity and quality.

For myself, I use the Pomodoro technique to help me with my work schedule. I usually block out about four hours of my day to work on my projects, be it writing or something else. I set the app's timer (you can easily download an app for this) to sound an alarm for twenty-five minutes of work, followed by a five-minute break, before getting back to another twenty-five minutes of work. This helps me to focus on the task at hand while giving me a mini-break at the end to look forward to.

> **Activity:** Review your main relationships, commitments, and projects at the moment. Do they conform to the 80/20 rule? In other words, are they giving you more joy and results than the time and effort you have put in?

Being selective—doing less—is the path of the productive.
Focus on the important few and ignore the rest.

—Timothy Ferriss

Stress bunnies are not adorable

Living well with less not only means living with fewer possessions that add value to our lives; it also means living with less strain on our mental and emotional well-being. When we feel unhappy, frustrated, worried, or stressed, it is a sign that what we are doing and where we are in life is not aligned with our happiness. It is a sign that we do not feel in control of our life and situations, that we have more than we can cope with on our plates.

The causes for these stressful situations often result from having too much stuff, money worries, stress from work, challenging relationships, or a general sense of being overwhelmed. Stress causes worry and vice-versa; both are unhealthy for our mental state. Stress impedes us from thinking and acting clearly; it is a hindrance to productivity and can shut down the creative, exploratory, and inquisitive part of our brain. It can also affect our health, relationships, and quality of life.

Like it or not, I believe stress is very much a part of our lives. While we can reduce it and get rid of unnecessary stress, it is quite impossible to live totally stress-free. Stress is caused by the challenges we face, and a life without challenges and the resultant growth is rather boring; it will make you stale. To overcome stressful or worrisome situations, we need to adjust our priorities to a place where things are better aligned with our happiness and peace of mind. This ideal place varies from individual to individual, and you will need to find out for yourself where your threshold is.

We all have our own list of things that cause us stress. I have listed some of these and explained how we can reduce or eliminate them. Stress reduction and elimination takes time to get a grip on, but little changes can make a significant difference.

Ways to reduce stress

Identify the sources of stress. Before we can deal with stress, we need to identify what causes it. Take a little time to list the top ten things/people/events/situations that cause you the most stress. Which are the ones that can be avoided, weeded out, or eliminated? For those that can't be gotten rid of, think of ways that you can work around them and make them less stressful.

Simplify. Henry David Thoreau was right when he exhorted us to "Simplify. Simplify. Simplify." A complex life filled with excess and multidimensional characters has a greater propensity for unknowns, uncertainties, difficulties, and errors. All these are stress inducers. So strip out the complexity and try to keep things simple as much as possible. It makes life easier.

Clear some space. Feeling overwhelmed causes us stress. This feeling can be triggered by having excess stuff, untidiness, and being overworked or too busy. We need to give ourselves the mental and physical space to breathe. So declutter your excess possessions and live with only what gives you joy and adds value. By putting things in their proper space, you will in turn clear spaces to live and work in. Review your commitments and activities, and only keep those from which you reap the most enjoyment and results.

Time for yourself. Don't forget to block out time for yourself to rest, relax, and rejuvenate. It could be just five minutes of doing nothing and being still, a ten-minute meditation session, or a thirty-minute workout session. Do whatever works to calm your mind and give you respite.

Set your own expectations and priorities. Expectations that are too high or insurmountable overwhelm us and stress us out. Expectations that are not met make us feel like failures. Set your own expectations rather than have them imposed upon you by others, as you know yourself best. You should also set your priorities and decide what is of the greatest importance to you; otherwise other people will prioritize your life for you, which can result in unhappiness and stress.

Focus on one thing at a time. As mentioned previously, multi-tasking not only causes stress, but also has a negative impact on productivity and the quality of the outcome. Focus on one task at a time and do it well before moving on to the next. It is also useful to focus and prioritize on tasks that deliver the most joy and significant results. Do not be afraid to say *no*.

Avoid stressful situations and people. Inevitably, we'll encounter situations and people that drain our energy. It could be our daily commute to work, crowded places, loud music, our job, our bosses, or our colleagues. Are there ways to reduce or avoid such situations and people? For example, if you find stress in your daily commute, try leaving earlier for work or leaving work earlier to avoid peak rush hour, or try taking another route. Learn how to manage difficult people, or eliminate them from your life altogether, if you encounter stress in your relationships. For many of us, our jobs probably cause the most stress. Do an honest review of your current job situation to see how well it serves you in terms of its benefits and trade-offs and how it is affecting your quality of life.

Be mindful. The concept of being mindful—being present and more conscious of life as it happens—seems daunting to many who live swinging from one task to another, pulled in various directions that require their attention. It seems that being mindful will impede one in accomplishing all of the tasks that need to be done, stopping life in its tracks. The opposite is true: being mindful will actually enable us to achieve our goals and live more fully and with greater intensity. By being mindful, you enjoy your food more, your relationships more, and anything else you are doing. Anything, even things that you might think are drudgery or mundane, such as housework, can become amazing. When we are mindful, we experience things as they are—in the present. We can't change the past or affect the future, but we can live in the now—and that gives us control. And when we feel we are in control, we will not be stressed.

Slow down. In this fast-paced world, we are exhorted to go faster and faster. For the sake of our well-being, we have to learn to do the opposite and slow down. Carl Honoré, the guru of the Slow Movement, puts it aptly: "By slowing down at the right moments, people find that they do everything better: They eat better; they make love better; they exercise better; they work better; they live better."

Learn to let go. We get stressed when we feel we are not in control—things might turn out badly and we'll be left in a disastrous situation. However hard we try to be masters of the universe, there are things we can control and many other things we can't. Learn to differentiate between things you can change and those you can't—learn to manage the former and let go of the latter.

Be an early bird. Being late can be stressful—especially for me! When I oversleep and wake up later than I planned, I feel my day is slipping away and being wasted. I'll get stressed and try to make up for it by doing more, and doing it quickly. In my previous life, when I was running from one meeting to another, I felt stressed when people were waiting, and I'd feel less prepared for the meeting as I wouldn't have the time to calm down and prep for the session. I have learned that getting an early start in the morning or getting to an appointment five minutes early makes a notable difference to my day and work.

Activity: Can you think of one thing that is the cause of the most stress in your life at the moment? What can you do to reduce or eliminate the stress?

Stress is caused by being "here" but wanting to be "there."

—Eckhart Tolle

Worrying does not get one anywhere

Worrying tends to go hand in hand with stress; the two feed off each other. While stress is driven by a sense of feeling overwhelmed and losing control, worry is mostly driven by fear. This is the fear of uncertainty, of the unknown, and of unwanted outcomes. When we visualize, we create an image in our mind of a future event and give it an affirmative and positive outcome. The opposite is true of worry, which is visualizing future failure and affirming that it will happen.

Our default mode of dealing with both the unknown and unwanted is to worry. We are always worried about what might go wrong, about what people think of us, about how things are going to work out, and so on. It is a natural tendency for us to focus on unwanted and negative outcomes. However, worrying does not add value nor provide any solution to our situation. It merely magnifies both the negativity and seriousness of the whole thing and its perceived outcome.

Just like stress, we can't eliminate worry totally from our lives; however, we can reduce it to the barest minimum.

Ways to reduce worrying

Acknowledge and face the fear. In most, if not nearly all, cases, worry is born out of fear. The default action would be to run away from fear, but no matter how fast or far you run, the fear will still creep up on you. The only way to reduce and eliminate that fear is to acknowledge its presence. There is no point in pretending it is not there; that is akin to an ostrich putting its head in the sand. Once you have acknowledged the fear and looked at it straight in the face, it might actually be less dreadful than you thought it was. When you can face your fears, you will be in a much better position to think of solutions and alternatives.

Have some faith. When dealing with worry, it is good to build up some faith and confidence in yourself and believe that you will be able to manage or come out with another option if things don't work out. There are usually alternative options open to us. Your confidence in finding a solution or ensuring that things will have the desired outcome will go a long way toward lessening your worries.

It is going to be okay. Can you remember the things that you were worried about in the past few days, months, and last couple of years? Most of them were probably little and insignificant things with no lasting impact on your life. In most of these cases, things turned out fine. Even if some of these situations had a negative outcome, your life did not fall to pieces.

It is always good to put things into perspective before being sucked into the worry spiral.

It is not the end of the world. One of the best ways to deal with worry and fear is to ask what is the worst that could happen. Usually, the answer is not as bad as we think it could be. Being presented with the worst-case scenario usually kick-starts our survival mode and spurs us on to think of ways to cope and solve the problem.

Activity: Can you think of your biggest fear in life at the moment? What can you do to reduce or eliminate this fear?

Worrying will never change the outcome.

—Anonymous

Take time out for yourself

When people or events take up our time, energy, and effort, we tend to forget the most important person in our life. The person without whom we would be nothing. That person is ourself. This is not some ego talk—you are indeed the most important person in your life, and you need to treat yourself well. Stuff can be bought and replaced and money can be earned, but there is only one of you and you are irreplaceable. Sometimes we forget that putting ourselves first is not selfish, but necessary.

Make it a priority to make time for yourself. Make time for rest, solitude, stillness, and doing nothing. Nothing else is more important than your well-being and peace. Happiness is unattainable if you have no space mentally, emotionally, and physically to breathe and grow. Fulfillment and financial freedom will come after you have put your own house in order and your energy and focus are centered. I have used the methods below to give myself rest and to reboot.

Five minutes of silence. Whenever I find myself feeling stressed and overwhelmed, I sit down somewhere quiet where I can be alone. I then close my eyes and stay still for five minutes. The quiet and stillness provides calm and clarity, helping me to return to what I was doing with renewed strength.

Ten minutes of meditation. Meditation has proven to be an effective way to provide peace and calm. You just need to find a place where you can be still and quiet. Breathe in and breathe out, noticing each breath as it enters and exits the body. Acknowledge any thoughts or feelings that come into your consciousness—and let them go. Keep the focus on your in-and-out breaths.

Fifteen minutes of getting away. Give yourself some space to breathe by doing something you enjoy. It could be making a cup of coffee or going out to get a cup of coffee, reading a chapter of a book, going for a quick walk around the block, and so on. When I had my nine-to-five job, I always made it a point to leave the office to get a coffee whenever I was feeling stressed or frustrated. Try to use this break to do offline stuff rather than checking your email or browsing the web or social media. Give your brain some time to switch off.

Activity: If you do not have the habit of making time for yourself, now is the time to start. Try to set aside a period of time for yourself to relax, reflect, or rejuvenate on a regular basis. It doesn't matter how long the period is, but make that time for yourself a priority.

Make time for yourself. You are important.

—Anonymous

Live with intention

When we talk about living life to the fullest, we are referring to experiencing it with a high degree of emotional excitement and depth of feeling. Unfortunately, for many of us, life is more like a rollercoaster ride of ups and downs rather than a constant high. And that is normal. Without lows, there would be no differentials and we would not appreciate the highs. Obviously, we would still prefer our life to consist more of highs than lows and to be able to use the time that we have to its fullest potential. To do so, we can live life with intensity by being more conscious and intentional.

Be in the moment. When we are conscious, aware, or present, we are in the moment. We don't reflect on the past or think about the future but are simply being here in the now. According to Eckhart Tolle in *The Power of Now,* many of us suffer from thought addiction. This is a condition where we are not present—and being present is actually a burden, something we can't wait to be done and over with. We see, but we don't really understand; we hear, but we don't listen (we were probably too busy formulating our own response!); we do work, but there is little sense of pride, craftsmanship, or creativity involved; we consume stuff without asking why;

we exist in our relationships or surroundings, but we don't truly appreciate them.

Next time you make a cup of coffee or tea, try slowing down and be aware of each step of the process. Take time to smell the aroma and taste the flavors and experience the sensations of imbibing it. You may find that you will enjoy and appreciate the drink so much more.

Reflect on your intention for the day. One of the first things I do at the start of each day is to have a short quiet period (I call it my quiet time), during which I reflect on my affirmations in life and the intention of my day. I believe that we should tell our day what to do instead of allowing it to happen to us. Since we are not in total control of everything, our day might consist of things or events that we might not feel good about. But there are also elements of your day that you do have control over. You get to evaluate the people and situations around you, pick your attitude, and make your decisions. Communicating our intentions to our subconscious gives our day a much better chance of turning out the way we want it to be.

Here is a simple practice of intentionality: before you perform your next action, pause for a moment and mentally verbalize your intention. Why are you doing this? What value or purpose does it serve? What is the desired outcome, and how will you feel once it has been done?

Activity: If you are not already doing so, make a start at "intentioning" your day and your daily tasks. Begin your morning with a few minutes of quiet time to visualize your day—the tasks you have to do and the people you'll meet. Visualize the desired outcomes. This will communicate to your subconscious how you would like your day—and your life—to pan out.

Energy flows where intention goes.

—Anonymous

Chapter 5:
Enhance Your Emotional Well-Being

Boosters and drainers

Earlier in the book, we mentioned that all things are made of energy—and they either boost or drain us. These could be emotions, people, situations, environments, the weather, food, the news, tasks and activities, colors, etc. It is important that we are conscious of what boosts our energy and what drains it. With low energy, we are depriving ourselves of the oxygen that enables us to live our life to the fullest.

I have listed ten things that boost my energy and another ten that drain it. It is worth making your own list, as this will give you a greater awareness of what helps you feel and perform at your optimum level—and what does the opposite.

My ten boosters
- Daily quiet time for both affirming and intentioning
- Living a curated and meaningful life
- Spending quality time with loved ones
- My morning coffee
- Reading a good book
- Exploring city streets
- Walking in nature
- Discovering and then working on inspiring, new business ventures
- Spending time in nice cafés and bookshops
- Interacting with like-minded people who share my values, ethos, and interests

My ten drainers
- Negativity
- Clutter
- Crowds and noise
- Loud music
- Watching TV mindlessly
- Reading and watching the news
- Spending too much time on social media
- Argumentative and unreasonable people

- Dull conversations
- Mundane work

Activity: Make a list of things that boost your energy and another list of things that drain your energy. Do more of the things in the former list, and avoid those on the latter list.

Do more of what makes you happy.

—Anonymous

Beware of the voids

Many of us have voids in our lives. These are left open as little pinholes or vast gaping crevices by a lack of something we crave. We seek to fill these voids in our lives with shiny new stuff, big houses and cars, impressive job titles, a good-looking person next to us, food, and media or entertainment. We can't fill these voids fast enough but they stay open, waiting for the next chunk of consumption. Open voids suck out our energy and hold us back. A void is merely a symptom. We need to look at the cause and understand what it is, before we can find the cure and fill the void. We need to look down and look deep at our voids, and see them for what they are. Only then can we fill them with the right stuff and keep them closed.

In addition to consumerism and materialism, comfort eating and excessive media consumption are two common manifestations of these gaping holes in our lives. We should see them for what they are: excuses and distractions from the real issues that are holding us back.

Comfort eating. Food is a delicious and warming fuel that provides us with sustenance and nutrition. However, like alcoholism, it gets confused with emotional states, such as reward, punishment, celebration, distraction, companion-ship, loneliness, sadness, bad habits, etc. It becomes a filler for the void in our lives by muting our sense of insecurity and low self-esteem; it fends off sadness, loneliness, and the pressing need to address an issue. Food does not judge us; it comforts us. Hence, it is so easy to want it—and to want lots of it.

Comfort eating is not going to fill the void. What it fuels is our false sense of security and procrastination. It delays the need to be honest with ourselves and with these gaps. Instead of being fulfilled, we need more of it to feel "full," and our bodies get bigger and unhealthier in the process.

Change your relationship with food and see food as nutrition and sustenance, not as a form of comfort and security. Practice conscious eating by consuming what you need, tasting each bite, and noticing the flavors and textures. Take your time to savor it and stop when you have had enough. Eat slowly. Give yourself the time to truly appreciate the food and listen carefully when your stomach tells you that it has had enough and warns you of overeating.

I find this Japanese philosophy, called *hara hachi-bu*, to be very useful for cultivating more mindfulness with food. It means "eat until you are 80 percent full." We can transform our health and relationship with food if we muster some self-control and mindfulness. Hara hachi-bu is based on a basic physiological principle: it takes your stomach's stretch receptors twenty minutes to tell your brain you are full, so if you eat until you feel 80 percent full and just wait twenty minutes, you will feel properly full.

Unconscious media consumption. Excessive and indiscriminate consumption of news (and most news today tends to be negative and draining), TV channel surfing, and obsessive checking of websites and social media are void fillers. They are unconscious actions to cover the gaps in our lives, as we attempt to push boredom, procrastination, loneliness, and a lack of purpose into the background by occupying our minds with something else. Many of us fear confronting the reasons behind this boredom and sense of emptiness. Distracting our monkey mind is so much easier and less painful. Meanwhile, the white elephant continues to stand in the middle of the room as we try our utmost to ignore it.

When I started simplifying my life and looking at what added value and what didn't, the news was the first to go. It mostly makes me feel like crap about the world and feeds negativity into my energy. As a believer of positive energy and that like attracts like, bad news is a big no. However, I am also aware that oblivion is not solely bliss; it can also breed ignorance.

So I have since derived a way of skimming the headlines and being roughly aware of what is going on without being sucked into the spiral of doom and gloom. More important, I have decided to curate the type and nature of news I get exposed to, ensuring that what I consume is informative. With these slight changes in news consumption, I see more beauty, kindness, and inspiration in people and the world around me. And that's positive!

The same goes for watching TV. I no longer own a TV, nor watch TV shows on a regular basis. However, I do watch the TV and movies that I enjoy from time to time whenever I need some entertainment.

Learn to be comfortable with yourself and your own presence. Have moments of silence where you can listen to the voice inside you and find out what you need. Is it a purpose in life? A meaningful relationship? A challenge to build yourself up? You don't always need to get rid of boredom—learn to be comfortable with it, as it can serve as a call for us to slow down and rest. To just be.

> *Life is 10 percent of what happens to you*
> *and 90 percent of how you react to it.*
>
> —Anonymous

Choose relationships that empower you

In our relationships and interactions with people, we have discovered that some people make us feel good. They support, inspire, and motivate us. When we spend time with them, we feel happier and energized—and we feel that we can be more. Then there are people who make us feel just the opposite. The effects of these interactions are magnified depending on whether we are extroverts or introverts, or a mixture of both.

According to the Myers-Briggs Personality Assessment, an extrovert increases her energy by interacting with the outer world of people, things, and events, while an introvert tends to be exhausted by these interactions and recharges through solitude and time alone. Hence, depending on the scale, relationships and interactions can either boost or suck your energy. More than that, depending on the kind of people we interact with, we can either feel uplifted or drained.

So, just as we are careful what we focus on in terms of our consumption, beliefs, and actions, we need to be aware of whom we choose to keep company with and their effects on our well-being. We should keep and nourish the positive relationships that empower us and discard the relationships that belittle and drain us. Make room for newly aligned relationships that inspire and help us to grow.

Start paying attention to how you feel in your various relationships and interactions. Do you feel happy, loved, inspired, supported, and empowered? Or do you feel negative, depressed, frustrated, exhausted, and made to feel that you are not good enough or a failure? You certainly would not want to be dragged down and held back by the latter group of people. They add little value to your quest for living a happier and fuller life.

Self-help guru Jim Rohn said, "You are the average of the five people you spend the most time with." You can interpret this in terms of beliefs, intelligence, achievement, wealth, and so on. Invest your effort and time on the people who build you up and do not put you down.

These are the types of people I tend to stay away from:

- People who are constantly negative, complaining, and moody
- People who constantly talk about themselves and are too self-absorbed to connect with others
- People who are argumentative and belligerent and would not even agree to disagree
- People who are ignorant and boring
- People who have no dreams or expectations and who are tired of life

This is not so much about avoiding people who have different values and views from oneself. Instead, it is more about whether these people, regardless of their values or views, make us question and grow through their different perspectives. At the end of the day, the heart of the issue is whether these differences challenge us positively and constructively—that is, broaden our thoughts and promote our growth—or if they simply pull us down with negative vibes and criticism.

Some relationships are more difficult than others to discard or stay away from. Family and relatives are one such example. The best way I have discovered is to be open and honest about how you want your life to be, and how their current behavior is not helping you move toward your desired state. Explain how you would like them to help and support you better. If they are open to your suggestions, great. If not, as we can't really disown them, we just have to choose to spend less time with them.

You can have the same honest discussions with friends who drain your energy. Give them a trial period of a few months to see if being around them can be a positive thing for you. If not, distance yourself and stop spending time with them. Do not feel guilty about losing such relationships. If you are honest with yourself, they do not add any joy or value to your life.

Fill your life with people who truly like you for who you are, who respect and encourage you and believe in your dreams.

Activity: Review the relationships in your life at the moment and put them into "positive," "room for improvement," and "negative" lists. Spend more time and effort with people on the positive list, seek improvement and common ground with those on the improvement list, and limit your time or disassociate with those on the negative list.

You can't change the people around you but you can change the people around you.

—The Minimalists

Reining in anger

Ellen Hopkins said that anger is a valid emotion; it's only bad when it controls you and pushes you to do things that you don't want to do. When people hurt us or when things don't go our way, we feel a wide range of negative emotions—hurt, fear, frustration, disappointment, jealousy, guilt, etc. These are primary emotions caused by the stimulus of things not going the way we wanted them to. Between stimulus and response, there is a space—a space to choose our reaction, and therein lies the opportunity for us to grow and be free, or be filled with regret and emotionally imprisoned. When we choose to respond with anger, when our mouths move quicker than our minds, it is a reaction and cover-up for the primary emotion that lies behind it. Anger is a secondary emotion.

Anger is both a survival tool as well as a source of energy. People who feel anger receive a shot of adrenaline and tend to perform beyond expectations—an angry person might begin to clean the house furiously or run like a leopard. There are productive ways to channel anger, and many have started inspiring movements or businesses because they were frustrated with the status quo.

At the other end of the spectrum, repressing our anger or holding onto it for prolonged lengths of time can be very damaging to our emotional well-being. Stifling our emotions will lead to either an external explosion or an internal implosion—or both. And that is something we should avoid.

Holding on to anger is like drinking poison and expecting the other person to die.

—Buddha

Our goal should be to increase the space between the stimulus and response. The space might roughly equate to the same time you would need to take a deep breath and count to ten. By doing this, we give ourselves more time to figure out what our primary emotion is and choose our response. I know, it is easier said than done. Here are a few ways I have learned to manage my own anger.

Take deep breaths. This sounds simple and unconscious enough, but sometimes taking a deep breath and being aware of doing such an "automatic" thing can be quite difficult when we are boiling with anger and just want to lash out. Before you tip over, take a pair of virtual scissors and, to use Pema Chödrön's phrase, "Nip your anger in the bud." Then breathe, and breathe deeply. The anger will probably still be there, but you will have saved yourself from its worst actions and reactions. In addition to taking deep breaths, leaving the source of the anger (person or space) and going elsewhere to cool down would also help to give the anger the space to dissipate.

Watch the triggers. When someone displeases us or when things don't work out the way we want them to, we feel a heat rushing upwards from our abdomen, blood concentrates in our head, and the default action is to lash out verbally or physically to release the built-up pressure. One way I have learned to cut down on my angry explosions is to notice and watch these triggers. When I notice my blood starting to boil, I acknowledge it and hold back before responding. I notice that even if I hold back for a mere two seconds, the delay makes a difference to my response. It gives me the space to detach myself and give more thought to my reaction and the potential consequences resulting from it. My response will probably still reflect my anger, but I can now frame it according to the primary emotion behind it. So, instead of screaming an insult, I might say, "What you said was really hurtful and this is how I feel about it . . ."

Expanding the envelope. This is a method shared by Leo Babauta of the blog *Zen Habits*. By widening the envelope of our perspective, from what we think is important to what the other sees as important, we might realize that they're having a difficult day, or that maybe life has not been treating them well, etc. It doesn't excuse their behavior, but it allows us to generate more empathy and compassion for them. In turn, this will help to moderate our anger and frustration. Some call this being "emotionally correct." Expanding the envelope can be challenging and difficult to do on a regular basis. But as we learn to be more aware and to watch our impulses before reacting, we will start noticing the gradual changes in our responses, and it will become more of a habit.

Activity: Do you remember the triggers or signs that prelude your angry outbursts? Try to pay attention to them before your next outburst, and see if you are able to better manage your anger.

The only cure for anger is delay.

—Seneca

Envy is a wasted emotion

We all get envious and jealous at one time or another, don't we? Actually, not everyone experiences envy or jealousy as an emotion—I'm one example. Why? Probably because somehow or other, over time, I have learned to accept myself for who I am and according to what I am capable of achieving. If I see someone with something I like or in a situation I would like to be in, instead of feeling envious, I tell myself I can have that or be that, too. I am lucky that I don't usually have to deal with envy or turning green.

Our society is riddled with envy and greed, the consequences of our competitive, materialistic, and consumer-driven culture. Envy is a by-product of competition, though packaged under more positive labels like "ambition" or "a competitive spirit." Envy breeds discontent, fuelled by certain cultural imperatives that we commonly refer to as "keeping up with the Joneses." Envy also extends beyond material things, such as being envious of someone's intelligence, or wondering, *Why is he spending more time with that other person instead of me?*

Though it is difficult or nearly impossible to get rid of envy, we can do it. Envy is a wasted emotion—it serves little purpose apart from making us feel inadequate and needy. Don't get me wrong—many negative emotions can serve a purpose: pain tells us something is wrong, fear tells us to look before we leap, and anger tells us that we are hurt and frustrated. However, envy doesn't help in any way; it merely broadcasts our insecurities. Below are a few things to stop the green monster from rearing its ugly head.

Be aware of your strengths. Whenever you feel yourself being tugged at by envy, be conscious of it and stop it in its tracks. Start focusing on your strengths and what you are already blessed with. We all have our own individuality and unique voice, and there is always something that will make us stand out. Pay more attention to what you already have and who you already are. You will be happier for it.

It is all relative. It is key to ask: who are we comparing ourselves against? There will always be people who are better than you and many who are worse off. We will have things that are the envy of others, and there will be people or situations who make us feel inadequate. It is an endless cycle, and we have to learn to be comfortable with where we are in the cycle. There are many winners and also many losers; it all depends on whom you are comparing yourself with.

Focus on the journey. Life is not a competition, it is a journey. Don't focus on where you rank in comparison to others; keep your eyes on your own path. We are all on a quest to be someone, learn something, and create something. Since it is a personal quest, where other people are going should have little bearing on us. We just need to worry about what we want to be, what we want to have, and where we want to go. That is all that matters.

Learn to love enough. Remember the concept of lagom—not more, not less, but just enough. We should keep that in mind when we want what others have. In an endless cycle, we will never have enough, and there will always be people who have more than us. Learn to appreciate that whatever you already have is enough—whether it is food, shelter, clothing, or loving relationships. If you are at peace with that, you will find contentment.

Live with imperfection. The world is not perfect; no one is perfect, and we will never be. Imperfection makes us who we are, and as described in the Japanese *wabi-sabi* principle, there is beauty in imperfection. We are already perfect as we are.

Celebrate the success of others. I know this can be hard. The common default reaction we have to other people's success is envy, followed by an evaluation of one's worth. But try to help and support others through their success, and you will find that you will grow as well.

> **Activity:** Are there any situations or people of whom you are envious? What are the causes of your envy? What can you do to reduce or eliminate the envy?

Enjoy your own life without comparing it with that of another.

—Marquis de Condorcet

Learning to let go

We tend to pin happiness on people and things that are familiar; and unhappiness tends to seep in when they are gone. We attach ourselves to feelings, even negative ones like fear and disappointment, and loathe the day when we have to give them up because their absence takes away our sense of security and comfort. We dwell in regret and unhappiness with replays of the should haves, would haves, and could haves.

Hanging on to stuff, people, and the past or hindsight is something many of us fall victim to. This attachment causes us much pain and regret. It is an impediment to our life moving forward and fulfilling its potential. If we don't let go of the things that are holding us back, life drags on, just like driving with the handbrakes on.

Look around you. Are there things, people, or situations that are holding you back? Excess possessions? Crappy relationships? A job you hate? Ask yourself, *What is the purpose of hanging on to it? Does it add any value to my life, and if not, what is stopping me from letting it go?*

Is it because this familiar situation is safe and comfortable? Or because society tells us it is the right thing to do? What if you just let go of the things that are holding you back? How would you feel to have a cleaner and less cluttered home?

Can you imagine not having to deal with feelings of low self-esteem, worry, and stress, and living instead with more peace and clarity? How about living with more time, money, and contentment?

An unwillingness and aversion to letting go wastes time and sucks up mental and emotional energy. It also limits our ability to experience joy in the moment. A moment can't be fully experienced if we are imprisoned by fear. When you stop trying to own and control the world around you, you give it the freedom to fulfil you without the power to destroy you. That's why letting go is so important: letting go is letting happiness in.

It is not an easy undertaking to let go of attachment. It's a conscious moment-to-moment, day-to-day commitment that involves changing the way you interpret, interact with, and experience the relationships and circumstances that you want to hang on to for various reasons.

So how do we learn to let go?

Be appreciative of the moment. Accept the moment for what it is. Don't dwell upon the past, speculate about the future, or worry about how you can make the present last. Enjoy it while it is here and now, before it becomes the past. Nothing is permanent. You might not be able to recreate your perfect day every day or be totally certain a relationship can last or situations will remain the same. So enjoy and appreciate what you have right now. Make now count. Focus on the quality, not quantity, of the experience.

Finding the core you. We change, people around us change, situations change. That is part and parcel of a constantly evolving and growing world. However, something in each of us is constant across all of these changes: when we define ourselves by our possessions, relationships, job titles, and so on, the loss of these attachments will result in not only losing what we own but also who we are as a unique entity.

To avoid that, define yourself in terms that will be a bedrock of constancy and that can withstand change. For myself, regardless of the changes within and beyond me, I will always be a pursuer of happiness, wealth, and simplicity—this way, my identity and purpose remain constant.

Question your attachment. If you are attached to a specific outcome—a desired level of wealth, the perfect relationship, a dream career—you may be indulging in an illusion about some future day when everything will be lined up for happiness. No moment will ever be worthier of your joy in the present because that is all there ever is. Live your meaningful life and fulfil your purpose now. Attach yourself to the pursuit of living well from moment to moment. That's an attachment that can do you no harm.

Love, not fear. When we hold on to the past, it is mostly because we fear making a mistake and not having the same opportunity again. When you fear, you worry. So, release the need to know everything, for life entails uncertainty. Focus instead on what you love, and create happiness.

Stay open to possibilities. Many of us have a problem with letting go because we have become comfortable with a situation—we fear that letting go will take away our security blanket. We cling to things and people we're comfortable with. We know how they will make us feel; whether it is happy, safe, familiar, or predictable. However, there is the possibility that allowing yourself into new things, relationships, and situations may provide you with the same feelings, if not more. The only way to find out is to let go and be open to new possibilities.

Learn to enjoy your own company. I love my own company, and I am comfortable with solitude (even though I also enjoy the company of others and am inspired by the people around me). Learning to be comfortable by yourself will make you less attached to the idea that you can only be happy if you are in various relationships, whether romantic, platonic, or familial. It makes you more self-reliant, and that is always a good thing.

Cultivate healthy relationships. Some of us tie our happiness and sense of worth to someone else's. We need that special someone or relationship to justify our existence, happiness, and success. If those relationships turn awry, then life will literally collapse. Hold lightly to relationships. Let them be healthy, rather than all-consuming. You are separate, and you are whole. You are not someone's other half. You can still hold someone close, but if you squeeze too tightly, both of you will suffocate. That's certainly not healthy! Also, try not to limit yourself to one or two relationships, as they will become your lifelines. Be open to new connections and possibilities.

No regrets. We all have replays of the should haves, would haves, and could haves. If you had known better, you would have done better. The fact that you feel guilty or regretful points to the gift of hindsight—you know better now and you have learned the lesson. If that's the case, it's time to move on. What is done cannot be undone. You can't change the past, but you can create your present and influence your future.

Pain is unavoidable. Pain is one of the few constants in life—until we reach the mythical nirvana, that is. At some point or another, we will lose things, people who matter to us, and situations that we were comfortable in. In a way, pain teaches us to appreciate the moment; it cautions us that nothing is permanent and that we need to be fluid and hang on lightly. Pain is inevitable, but suffering is optional.

Change your story. Vocalizing and writing things down both help to release the stuff we need to let go. It is therapeutic. It is also useful to change the story that we tell ourselves. In the story, we are able to redefine what something, someone, or some event meant to us and internalize what we learned, including if and how it has benefited us. Telling your story puts things into perspective and makes the letting go easier and less painful.

> **Activity:** Are there any things or situations you are hanging onto in your life right now that you find difficult to let go? What are the reasons you are hanging onto them?
>
> What can you do to let them go, slowly and one at a time, in order to let joy and lightness into your life?

Accept what is. Let go of what was.
Have faith in what will be.

—Anonymous

Going with the flow and taking inspired action

I find that learning to go with the flow is one of life's most underrated skills. There is nothing wrong with making an effort—it is what keeps us moving and growing and producing. But there is an "unnatural" element about it when that effort requires struggle. It drains our energy and is against what might be in our best interests.

If your lifestyle does not come naturally, if your relationships and work are a constant struggle, and if you keep coming up against obstacles that test your best perseverance, you are going against the flow. Your life is moving backwards instead of forwards. Going against the flow drains one's energy as you resist, struggle, deny, justify, repress, and fight. It is probably a sign that whatever you are living or fighting for is not really you or meant for you. Continuing your struggle will only create more unhappiness and frustration. So, save your energy, find your purpose, unleash your passion, and go with the flow.

The greatest level of freedom is being at one with the Universe, of being part of its "flow." This is similar to the Taoist concept of *wu wei*, which literally means "not doing." It doesn't mean that we should do nothing, but that we should put up no resistance to the natural energy of things—to just *be*.

This might mean different things to different people. It is like water flowing over a rock in a stream—both act in different ways, but most important, they are acting naturally. The water is acting like water and the rock is acting like a rock; neither needs to expend any energy in achieving this natural state.

By forcing things along and trying to make things happen, we usually end up worse off and nowhere closer to our goal and destination. For example, I have been trying to write a blog post over the last couple of weeks, but hours spent sitting in front of my laptop have produced very little. However, I woke up today feeling inspired to write a post, took action, and the post was written in a short time with little effort. The same is true when I find myself scratching my head for new ideas and projects to work on. I have learned to let go and go with the flow. When the time is right, the ideas will come without me looking for them. Learn to embrace inspired action, rather than struggle with forced or reactive action.

> *By letting it go it all gets done. The world*
> *is won by those who let it go. But when you try and try,*
> *the world is beyond the winning.*
>
> —Lao Tzu

Gratitude opens the door to contentment

If I were to present a blank sheet of paper with a black dot right in the middle of it and ask you what you see, your answer would probably be *a black dot.* What many fail to see is the whole ocean of white surrounding the black dot. We tend to go on about what is wrong with our lives, neglecting to be grateful for what is well with it. The same case can be applied to customer feedback. Few bother to give good feedback, but many more are motivated to complain about what isn't right. At the heart of people seeing more bad than good, or more lack than sufficiency, is a sense of discontent.

Discontent feeds unhappiness because we feel our situation could be much better. It fuels materialism and excess consumption as we are dissatisfied with what we already have, and it feeds our substance dependence habit as we are displeased with our current state of being. But channeled into the right and positive channels, discontent can also serve as a motivator for change and growth.

Meanwhile, the opposite of discontent is content; and the way to contentment is gratitude. Being content requires us to be aware of the good around us, and gratitude is the acknowledgment of this goodness. Having gratitude requires us to focus on the good things, relationships, and situations that we already possess and have a greater appreciation of them. By doing so, we in turn give less attention to what is not so good. In fact, being grateful simply reduces the space for discontentment to thrive, increasing the chances for happiness to take root.

Before I became a minimalist, I was seldom grateful, even though I owned a lot more stuff, because I felt there was always something else I needed or wanted despite the abundance that surrounded me. I own much less stuff now, and I feel a lot more grateful for what I have. I'm more conscious of why these things are in my life and the value they provide.

Grateful people are happier people, as shown by numerous scientific studies. They tend to enjoy increased well-being, healthier lifestyles, increased optimism, and a more positive outlook on life. In addition, those who display a high level of gratitude are much more likely to have below-average levels of materialism.

The expression of gratitude cuts across one's circumstances. Living in London, I have met people who have various levels of financial wealth and are from all walks of life. Some tend to be grateful, no matter how much or how little they have. Others complain, no matter how much they have, and those with less complain even more. I have traveled to First World countries where people enjoy a good quality of life, yet the level of happiness is not reflected in the level of abundance. I have also been to less developed countries where, despite the scarcity and lack of modern luxuries, most people have managed to adapt and enjoy what little they have. When I was in Bali, I saw groups of children making time for hearty conversations, laughter, and games along the beach, in between selling homemade bracelets to tourists. They had no branded clothes, phones, or iPads, but at that particular moment, I saw unbridled joy and carefreeness.

I try to make gratitude a daily habit by listing three things I am grateful for first thing in the morning, and another three things I am grateful for before I go to sleep at night. It helps me to start and end my day on a more positive note. During the day, I also try to notice things that make me feel fortunate—these help to keep unhappiness and discontent at bay.

No matter our situation or station in life, there are bound to be things we are grateful for. If we do not appreciate the little things, we will still see the lack when the bigger things come our way and will be confined to a cycle of lack, discontent, and unhappiness. If nothing else, be grateful for life—a finite span of time with infinite possibilities.

Activity: Make a habit of noticing and appreciating what you have and what is going well in your life. Start the day by listing three things you are grateful for, and do the same before you go to bed at night.

It is not happy people who are thankful.
It is thankful people who are happy.

—Anonymous

Chapter 6:
Financial Well-Being
Is Freedom

Money is many things, but not everything

Most would say that the primary purpose of life is generally to be happy. Money goes some way toward facilitating and enabling that happiness. It could be paying for that roof over our head, nice clothes to wear, outings at good restaurants, that trip to see the Grand Canyon, the college degree that will give us a step up in life, or a little gift to cheer someone up. Money is crucial and pervasive in many areas of our society. Unless one's life is self-sufficient or one can rely on barter trade, no one can really escape from the money-driven economy.

Minimalism is not anti-consumption; it is instead being more aware of it and questioning it. Similarly, the desire to live well with less is not against having money or having more of it. Remember that a minimalist lifestyle should be a joy and not a deprivation.

The main thing is to recognize what money is and what it is not. We go through life with various perceptions of money, some right and some wrong, some healthy and others not. As in all things, to make money work for us, we need to have a positive and healthy relationship with it. To do this, there are three main things we need to know and internalize about money.

Money is a means to an end. Money is just something that we ascribe value to in order to serve as a legal tender for the exchange of goods and services. When people say they love money, what they are actually saying is that they love the power of money and what it gives them in terms of status, security, goods, and services. Money is a tool and a means to an end; it serves as a recognized form of exchange to get what we need and desire. Hence, we should master money and make it work for us, rather than being a slave to it. Money is a poor master, but a good slave.

Money is neither good nor evil. Many of us grew up with the perception that money is evil and that having too much of it is going to corrupt us. Such views take the wrong approach. Remember: money is merely a tool, a means to an end. It is neither good nor bad. It is what we do with money that matters and determines whether we have put money to good use or not. Just as one should not be ashamed of being poor, there is nothing to shout about being poor either; there is no virtue in poverty. Poverty entails deprivation, and it usually brings about worry, stress, and nonfulfillment. That is not a joy and not what minimalism is about.

Money is energy. Like all things, money is energy. If one thinks that money does not come easily and that having money is bad, then guess what? With that kind of negative energy you are unlikely to see much money coming into your life. Like attracts like, and hence it is important that we have the right perception and relationship with our financial tools. Embrace money for its value and usefulness, and aim to have enough to meet your needs and provide peace of mind.

> **Activity:** What are your current beliefs about and relationship with money? Are these beliefs healthy and are they helping or obstructing you from achieving your financial well-being and goals?

Money is not the only answer, but it makes a difference.

—Barack Obama

Time is our most precious resource

Life is unfair. We are born into families and countries of various degrees of prosperity. Some of us are born better looking or healthier than others, some have gifts and talents that others would love to have, some are blessed with opportunities that will give their life that extra boost . . . the list goes on. However, we all have one thing that we share in equal measure. Regardless of our wealth or talent, we are given the same amount of time in a day: the sixty seconds in a minute, the sixty minutes in an hour, and the twenty-four hours in a day. Money, talent, or a Rolex will not buy you more time.

Time is the most precious resource we have. It is absolute and limited. You cannot owe a debt to time. If you spend more time on someone or something than you really wanted to, that time is taken from something else. Money can be earned, but we cannot have more than the twenty-four hours that we are given. That is why spending time with somebody might be one of the most precious things you can give because once time is used, you can't earn it back. Spending money on clutter is one thing, because money can be replaced. But spending time to make that money and *then* spending it on clutter is using up our most precious and irreplaceable resource.

How we enhance our use of time is the one thing that will give purpose, meaning, and value to our lives. No matter the status of your birth or your current situation, what you focus on and how you invest your time will be the key determinant in how meaningful and successful your life will be.

Accept life for what it is—a finite span
of time with infinite possibilities.

—The Minimalists

Maximizing the minimalist budget

Minimalism is about discovering what you need and what is essential to your happiness and well-being, and fulfilling that need exactly. Minimalist budgeting is about understanding what you need in order to have enough and the optimal way you can allocate your resources to that end. In our society, where excess is the norm, we tend to forget that to have exactly enough is not suffering or deprivation.

The aim of any regular budget is to allocate our limited monetary resources in such a way as to balance our income with expenditure, maximizing the efficiency of each dollar and keeping us from spending more than we have and going into debt. To budget well, one must either spend less or make more money.

Minimalist budgeting is like regular budgeting, but with an added emphasis on what is truly important to you. In addition to planning and watching the dollars and cents, we are also looking at which items of income and expenditure add value and contribute toward your happiness, so you can allocate more resources to them accordingly. At the same time, we cut out our expenditure on nonessentials and items with little effect on our well-being.

While thriftiness and being money-conscious are excellent skills to have and absolutely necessary for some, minimalist budgeting is more about conscious decision-making. It is not about stinginess and trying to endure a lack, although I recognize that some people will need to endure penny-pinching times in order to get their finances back in order. Remember: minimalism should be a joy and not a deprivation. The primary purpose of your life is to be happy. But if you are maximizing your money to the point where you are less happy, your budget is no longer serving its purpose.

In other words, the key to successful minimalist budgeting is to maximize our happiness, minimizing the amount of resources that we need to allocate in terms of money, time, effort, and energy to achieve this goal. It is not so much about frugality as it is about efficiency. It is about making your dollar stretch further, and more important, it asks you to examine what that dollar means to you. A budget is more meaningful and more effective if it takes into account your need to be financially and spiritually fulfilled.

Oscar Wilde's advice seems particularly relevant and prescient: "When you only have two pennies left in the world, spend one on bread and the other on a lily." He understood something about budgeting and value. He valued not only his need to eat but also his own inspiration, his own sense of well-being, and believing the world is a beautiful place.

> *The goal isn't more money. The goal is living life on your terms.*

—Chris Brogan

The three components of a minimalist budget

1. **Money.** In a regular budget, there is only one key component: money. We look at how much income we have and how much expenditure we are chalking up, and try to find a balance between the two so that our expenditure is within the income. Money can be earned, but there are limits as to what we can earn and how little we spend.

2. **Time.** A minimalist budget actually begins with time rather than money. Time is nonnegotiable—you have twenty-four hours a day and seven days a week. The basis for all work is the trading of time for money. You sell a piece of your time through the work and effort you put into it in exchange for income. This works out fine if you intend to use that money to enrich the remaining time you have, but sadly people tend to forget about the balance between time and money, and they make choices as if time is infinite and money is most important.

3. **Value.** The subjective value that we assign to both money and expenditure items is the only component missing from most regular budgets, and that is also the one we have full ownership and control over. A simple way to find out how to factor value into your life is to ask how

much value each item adds to your well-being. You will then find out what really matters to you, regardless of their market worth or the time invested.

For example, if you love books, you might spend 30 percent of your income on buying books and nearly all of your free time reading them. But if they give you immense joy and satisfaction and are an accurate reflection of the value they add to your life, they should remain in your budget. You might even consider allocating more money and time to them. If reading is not that important to you, it will not be a big loss for you to reduce the amount of resources allocated to it. Remember, we are not trying to remove every expenditure item that does not contribute to your basic survival and well-being. We are just trimming away the nonessentials and clutter items so that we are free to dedicate our time and money to what really makes us happy.

> *Nowadays, people know the price of everything but the value of nothing.*
>
> —Oscar Wilde

A minimalist budget that works for you

We have explored the ethos behind a minimalist budget and how its primary purpose is to enhance your happiness and well-being. It is defined both by conscious spending and efficiency. It is not about removing everything, only those things that are unnecessary and that do not add value to your quality of life. Now let us craft out your own minimalist budget. You can do this by taking the following steps:

1. **List all income and expenditure.** The first thing to do is to get an idea of the current status of your financial situation. For simplicity's sake, let's focus on the income and expenditure for a month. Identify all your income streams and add them up. Do the same with all expenditure items. If you don't have the exact figures for all of the items, give them an estimated value. Compute the difference between total income and total expenditure. Are you spending within your income or beyond it? If it is the former, the goal is to see if you can reduce your expenditure by cutting out the nonessentials and focus on getting more value out of your budget. If it is the latter, the goal is to try to live within your income and reduce debt. It will obviously also

include cutting out various expenditure items that are not essential to your well-being.

2. **Get rid of the fluff.** This is what I call the first cull of budgeting. Go through your expenditure items that are nonessential. For example, subscriptions to magazines you no longer read or direct debits to services you no longer have a need for and items that you barely know or remember. You are paying for them on a regular basis. Since you hardly use or even remember them, you will not miss them. They all need to go.

3. **Comb through what's left.** Now run though the remaining essential items and see if there is any nonessential expenditure hidden among them. Remember, your essential list will probably include items like mortgage or rent, utility bills, savings and investments, clothing, groceries, transport, and other items that serve a purpose or add value to your life. These will vary from individual to individual, according to needs and preferences. For someone who is very social, for example, expenditure for eating out and partying will be an essential item.

Next, comb through your list of essentials and see if you are on the best deal on items like mortgages, savings and investments, utilities, and phone and broadband deals. From my personal experience, companies will usually be the first to notify you about any increase in fees but see little reason to let you know if you could be on a better deal and pay less due to your customer loyalty or usage behavior. It is certainly worth doing some research and making some calls to your service providers to make sure you are on the best possible deal. You will be surprised how much money you could save just by doing a bi-annual or annual review of these items.

4. **Money investment.** We are going to look at how much resources are invested on essential expenditure items. Assign a percentage to each expenditure item as part of the total income. For example, if your total income is $1,000 and your mortgage costs $300, then the percentage assigned to your mortgage will be 30 percent.

5. **Time investment.** Now do the same for the time you spend working or enjoying each of the expenditure items. Assign a percentage to each expenditure item as part of total time. For example, if you had 100 hours, how many of those hours would you be working to pay your mortgage? If it is 40 hours, then you will assign 40 percent of time to your mortgage.

6. What's the value add? We measure value add in terms of not just how important that expenditure item is on our list, but also if the resources toward it have been allocated in the most efficient manner in meeting our needs and adding value to our life.

Let's look again at the mortgage example. If the mortgage takes up 30 percent of your income and you invest 40 percent of your time working to generate the income to pay for it, are you getting a fair return in terms of happiness, satisfaction, and comfort from it? If not, look to adjust the amount of money and time spent toward it. This might involve paying a higher mortgage for a better place that will make you happier or looking for a more affordable place that you won't have to allocate so much of your resources toward, and divesting the money saved toward other needs.

I have a friend who, like me, is very house proud and spends a good portion of her time enjoying her home. She spends roughly 40 percent of her income on her mortgage and about 50 percent of her time working to pay for it. But she gets a huge amount of joy from her home, so that's a good and positive value add. I have another friend who spends most of her time eating out and partying, and so she made a decision to rent a cheap one bedroom in a shared house and allocate most of her resources and time to what gives her most joy: socializing and spending time outside of her home.

7. **Note the essentials that are not in the budget.** At this juncture, it is important to pay attention to items that are important in our lives but are not reflected in the budget. These might include time for yourself and your loved ones, or doing things that you enjoy. If we spend too much time generating an income and paying for various expenses, we will probably not have as much time and energy as we would like to devote to our loved ones and hobbies we are passionate about. It would then make sense to see if we need to review our expenses to reduce our financial commitments or look at how we can generate income more efficiently, both with a goal to allocate more time to the things that matter most to us.

8. **Economic rent.** There is a concept in economic theory called "economic rent." It is any pay over the minimum amount that is acceptable for doing a job. When you decide what you are going to do for the rest of your life, go for the activity with the highest economic rent.

However, take a smaller pay check if a job is going to give you happiness instead. Nothing that compensates you with a big pay check will make up for the misery of doing a job you hate, Monday through Friday.

Activity: Draft up a minimalist budget to get a better idea of your current happiness-financial status.

Are you happy with it? If not, what steps can you take to improve it?

When things aren't adding up in your life, start subtracting.

—Anonymous

Mindful consumption

In order to get our financial house in order, we have to either make more money or spend less. As a minimalist, we do not eschew consumption. Rather, we are mindful as to what we consume. Before letting anything into our lives, we ask if it adds value, serves a purpose, or gives us joy. Mindful consumption means having our principles firmly in place before we consume or purchase anything.

Since embracing minimalism, I've saved both time and money. I shop less as I have less need for stuff. I also spend less time per shopping trip as I have a clearer idea of what I'm looking for.

When you are conscious and know what you are buying and why, you are somewhat immune to advertising. If not, you are basically letting the forces of marketing take your money away from you. If you practice mindful consumption, you are consuming as a conscious choice and decision rather than being influenced into consumption, which usually leads to buying things we do not need. Apart from choosing to consume only what you need and what brings you joy, put more value on quality—and don't be swayed by discounts and sale prices. If you are tempted to value quantity over quality, Benjamin

Franklin's quote might help: "The bitterness of poor quality remains long after the sweetness of low price is forgotten."

It helps to have a plan before heading out to shop, so keep it simple, review the options, and keep your needs and resources in mind. Don't compare yourself with others. Just because someone wears a certain brand doesn't mean that it is suitable for you. Don't give your money to brands and shops that spread the message you are not good enough unless you wear X and consume Y. Avoid shopping when you feel tired, sad, or bored, as advertising speaks to your weakness and emptiness. Just like comfort eating, you will likely end up buying more than you need.

> *The cost of a thing is the amount of life which is required to be exchanged for it, immediately or in the long run.*
>
> —Henry David Thoreau

Debt-free living

A key reason for my adoption of a minimalist lifestyle is to be free—to experience and enjoy a sense of lightness and to be open to the options and possibilities that come with freedom. Just as I have never forgotten how I felt the moment after completing the major declutter of my possessions, I have also never forgotten the lightness that washed over me when I became debt-free. Living debt-free has loads of benefits, but at the end of the day it is a personal decision that is based on how you want to live your life and your priorities.

Since I embraced simple living and minimalism, I started a blog, *Simple and Minimal* (simpleandminimal.com). A draft post entitled "I am debt-free" had always been at the top of my list to be completed, written, and published. Two years after I started the blog, I was finally in a position to write such a post: I am debt-free, and I have money in the bank. I couldn't believe it. It felt rather surreal, and even after two months it hadn't yet fully sunk in.

For the first time since I left university, I was totally free of debt. Debt-free: a word that seems so innocuous, yet whose attainment can bestow so much freedom, lightness, and control. The freedom to explore options, make choices, and pursue dreams. The lightness that comes with not owing a single penny and owning every single dollar, beholden to no one but myself. The control I regained over my finances and my time and how I wanted to spend them. The realization that I fully own every one of my possessions and assets. That feeling is rather indescribable.

Many of us have debts in one form or another, and in varying amounts, once we reach adulthood. University debts, credit card debts, car loans, and mortgages are all part of being grown up and getting ahead. We are mortgaging our future for a better present, which we can't presently afford; in the hope that our future will be able to cough up the payments. Then that opportunity arises for that nicer suit, that newer car model, and that bigger house, and we fall deeper into the debt hole.

One would hope that job promotions and pay raises would make our lives a little easier and our debt pile a little smaller, but this is easier said than done. With more money, we yearn for that even nicer car and bigger house to keep up with our newly elevated status. Oh dear, we just have to stay in that crappy job for a little while longer to keep up with the payments. Having money can make us poorer and more indebted—sad but true. It is like buying bigger-sized pants to accommodate our bigger waistline, but ending up eating more because we now have more room to fill!

We all consume in one way or another, and I am not saying consumption is bad. We all need shelter, food, clothing, and a few other things to make our lives comfortable, enjoyable, and efficient. But mindless consumerism, where we consume impulsively and with the vain hope that it will give us the happiness and purpose we crave for, is self-defeating. It is likely to make us more reliant on the jobs we loathe and leave us further from our true happiness and purpose.

I followed a similar trajectory after university. I had good jobs that earned me good pay with good companies in exchange for long hours, stress, and diminishing personal time and self-fulfillment. Weekends were sacred as I sought to spend those precious hours doing things I liked and spending money on things I wanted in order to assuage the misery that piled up during the work week and dull the dread of heading back to the grind on Monday. Sunday night blues are not just a myth; it was very real and tangible in my case. Each new job and promotion delivered more money into my bank account, but there never seemed to be enough for me to feel "rich," even though I was supposedly among the top 10 percent of income earners in London.

I was buying stuff; not only things I needed, but also things I *thought* I needed and wanted. I used to think that if I were to leave the house, I needed to bring something back—anything, even a copy of the day's papers to make it worthwhile, even though I didn't have the desire nor the time to read them. I was buying stuff on my holidays and work trips, and so each overseas posting added more to my possessions. Even though anyone walking into my apartment would find it nice and tidy and nowhere near cluttered, *clutter* can be a rather subjective term. I had a lot more stuff than I actually needed or wanted, and it was draining my finances, robbing me of my time, and clogging up my living space. I was buying stuff with my hard-earned money and credit cards, hoping to numb the misery of my cubicle existence. I was staying in the job so that I could fund my purchases and pay off my bills, getting the next bigger job with a bigger pay check and consuming more to numb the bigger dose of misery and dullness that came with it. The cycle repeated itself. But the happiness remained ephemeral. I spent more money and had less time and control over my life.

While my jobs paid the bills and indulged me with the little luxuries in life, they left me empty. With time, the misery grew deeper and the emptiness reverberated stronger. I finally took the plunge and left the corporate world to spend my time working on projects I was passionate about, projects that awarded my life with purpose and value. I felt a lot happier, freer, and more fulfilled. But I still carried the burden of having to pay the bills and think about making a living. Then I chanced upon a blog post by The Minimalists entitled "Debt-Free," and I was blown away. It was as if the scales had dropped from my eyes and a stone was lifted off my back. I was filled with hope, excitement, and lightness—clichéd, but true. This was the carefree state I wanted to be in: debt-free. Saying is much easier than doing, and my path toward being debt-free was a long, drawn-out process with tough decisions and plenty of uncertainties. But I finally made it, and I am truly embracing the freedom that came with the disentanglement.

Below is an extract of that blog post I wrote after I became debt-free:

I am writing this post in one of my favorite local cafés. A light-filled space staffed by friendly baristas that serves great coffee and Eccles cakes by St. John (the best ever!). I paid for my coffee and cake with cash, as I do with the bulk of my purchases. I seldom use my debit card nowadays. My two credit cards have not left my wallet in the past two months and have become seemingly redundant. Cold hard cash gives me better control over my spending and prompts me to buy and consume more mindfully. I also tend to ask myself if a purchase is going to add value to my life and be worth that amount of money to my freedom and time. I glance through the list of properties that are up for sale. The London property boom has thrown up a slew of properties that are way overpriced, waiting for desperate buyers rushed by the limited supply to take the bait. I believe that I will find my dream home—one that is right for me, when the time is right. I guess one can't rush such things; magic happens when you are least expecting it. When that dream abode turns up, I will be paying for it in cash—no more mortgages, no more debt.

I turn my attention to Helen, the barista. Watching her make coffee is quite addictive: grind the beans, fill the porter holder and slot it into the machine, press the button, and watch as the coffee gets extracted into the cups, sending wafts of coffee aroma my way. I have always had a keen interest in coffee and have recently taken it up a level by attending coffee courses. The thought of opening my own bookshop and café has always been lurking at the back of my mind; waiting for the right moment to manifest itself into reality. I can afford to buy my own shop now. That is if I wanted to. I can also work as a barista and make beautiful coffee all day long if I wanted to. Being a barista had never been an option for me in the past because I needed to "make a good living" in order to pay my bills and maintain my standard of living. But now, being debt-free has opened me up to choices and options, and I am free to choose and pick the road I want to travel on. There is nothing to hold me back except myself.

You can find the above post and other posts related to simple living and minimalism on my blog, *Simple and Minimal* (simpleandminimal.com).

> *Home life ceases to be free and beautiful as soon as it is founded on borrowing and debt.*
>
> —Henrik Ibsen

Living and staying debt-free

There are good debts and bad debts. Some people consider all debt to be bad and do not touch it with a barge pole. Like minimalism, one's perception and relationship with debt is personal and individual. The key questions to ask are: How much, if any, debt are you comfortable with? Is it keeping you awake at night and causing you stress? Is your debt stopping you from living the life that you want? For example, are you tied to a job that you dislike and prevented from doing what you love because that job pays your bills and debts?

If you are comfortable with having some kind of debt and see it as necessary for certain things in life, stay with having good debts. These will probably include an affordable mortgage for a house and student loans to facilitate further education and the acquiring of new skills. Apart from these two items, any other debt, such as credit card debt and unsecured personal loans, are considered bad and to be treated with caution. Personally, since I got rid of my mortgage, I have made a conscious decision to buy my next home in cash and to live totally debt-free. Anything that I need or want will have to be financed from my own money.

So how does one reduce debt and live debt-free? I am sure there are personal finance books out there that will provide a more detailed and thorough debt reduction and elimination plan. But I have listed a couple of things that might get you started on reducing and getting rid of that debt pile.

Mindful consumption. If you have followed us on the minimalism journey and read the previous chapters, you would have understood the importance of asking the "Does this serve a purpose or add value to my life" question. Before purchasing anything, you would be more aware and deliberate. When you only buy things you truly love or need, you will reduce your spending, and, in the process, reduce your debt, if you have any.

Have a plan and stick to it. Like most projects, you need a plan to make sure that all of your resources are allocated in the most effective and efficient way. Getting rid of debt is no exception. First, find out how much you owe in total and to whom. Then pay them off in terms of priority. Some people find it more motivating to pay off the credit card with the least debt first, and pay the minimum on the rest of the cards. Others find it more efficient to pay off the card with the highest interest rates first and work their way down the list. There are also people who find it useful to consolidate all their debt and devote a chunk of their income toward paying it off. There is no right or wrong way to do it; pick the method that works best for you.

Once you have a plan, do not be distracted or seduced. Keep the focus on reducing debt and throw as much money as you can afford toward paying it off as soon as possible.

Throw any extra cash toward paying off your debt. Debt elimination is a commitment and requires a good deal of determination and discipline. When you have some extra cash left over, you might be tempted to buy that beautiful sweater you saw in the shop window the other day. Stop and think: do you want that sweater bad enough that you are willing to remain in debt slavery for longer?

If you are really serious about getting rid of your debt, you have to give your all and chuck nearly, if not all, your extra dollars and cents at it. The earlier you pay off your debt, the earlier you will be free. Yes, reward yourself with a little something or pat yourself on the back for the job well done, but make sure you pay in cold hard cash and not add it to the debt pile.

Activity: Do you have any debts? If so, are they helping you to achieve your dreams or are they holding you back from your dreams?

Debt is the slavery of the free.
—Anonymous

Chapter 7:
Crafting and Curating an Extraordinary Life

Giving meaning to life

If I were to ask you what would you do if you struck the lottery jackpot, you would probably say something like pay off your debts, buy your dream home and car, share it with your loved ones, donate some of it to charity, or quit your job and turn your life into one never-ending holiday. All lovely ideas, especially the one about being on holiday forever. Then what?

You see, I have tried going to the beach for a month, just doing nothing. The skies were blue, the weather was warm, the ocean was beautiful, the trees were swaying gently, and I practically had the whole sandy white beach to myself. I was truly living the life of an idler, an Inspired Idler, as I like to call myself. That is, idle with a purpose instead of simply doing nothing. It was lovely for a week—and then I got a little bored. I didn't have time or financial constraints during my holiday, but I began to want more from it after a while.

Could it be too much of a good thing? Or might it be that we tend to seek something more in life, some deeper meaning and purpose to our existence? We have all read the statistics about how having money makes your life easier, but it doesn't necessarily make you happy. We all have our own definitions of what makes us happy and fulfilled. It might be money for some, but remember: money is merely a means to an end. For others it might be buying a home, running a successful business, working in a dream job, finding a soul mate, or contributing to the happiness of others.

At the basic level, we all want to feel that what we do is a part of something bigger than us. The world is vast, and we are just one little itsy-bitsy blip in the whole scheme of things. We would all like to have given off some light and made a difference, no matter how little, during our short and finite time in the world. Finding one's purpose and meaning in life can happen in any context, if you have the right mindset.

After I left my corporate job, I went on a long "sabbatical" holiday with the aim of thinking up new business ideas—projects that I enjoyed working on that would provide purpose to my days and some kind of meaningful framework to my life. I ended up on that beach, and achieved little during my days of lazing around doing nothing. When my holiday was nearing its end, it finally hit me that the business idea I had been looking for was right under my nose the whole time.

Sometimes we go away to find answers, only to realize that the answer is not what we had expected—and sometimes it is already present in our lives. What had brought me out of my restlessness was not more leisurely idleness, but the realization that I wanted to make a contribution—I wanted to work on something that could provide a meaning and purpose to my life; something that could add value. We all do. It is not just the work that fulfils us; it is the reason behind our work that does as well.

Currently, much of psychology says that human motivation is about seeking pleasure. However, according to the acclaimed psychologist Viktor Frankl, what we really seek is meaning, and the way we find it is not by numbing ourselves with substances or drowning ourselves in stuff, but by doing something that matters. For Frankl, this belief in the importance of meaning was what kept him alive while imprisoned in Nazi concentration camps during the Second World War. It was the book he was writing and the hope that he had of seeing his wife that enabled him to endure the hardship and pain.

What gave me a renewed sense of purpose was something that aligned with my passion and that would also allow me to contribute beyond myself. The answer was minimalism. Minimalism had transformed my life, and I wanted to share its benefits with others. I had been writing a blog about my minimalism journey for a few years, and I decided to build upon it and invest my time and resources in a venture (livewellwithless.com) that would inspire and help others to live more with less. This book is one of the outputs of the venture. Doing what I like is freedom; liking what I do is happiness. The big win is to discover, create, and connect out of a deep and authentic sense of who I am—a venture that is profitable, enriching, and sustainable.

We all have a purpose, a task for which we were designed, and the goal of your life is to find it—not somewhere out there, but rather hidden in the life you are already living. To paraphrase Frankl, we don't want to just be happy; we want a reason to be happy. And if you can embrace that truth, you've already won the lottery.

> **Activity:** Have you found your purpose and meaning in life? If not, think about who and what makes you happy and gives you enjoyment. Are these people and things enough to provide some meaning to your life and a sense of purpose to your days?

The purpose of life is to discover your gift. The work of life is to develop it. The meaning of life is to give your gift away.

—David Viscott

Crafting your mission

So how can we live a more meaningful life? What are our values, goals, and dreams that will make our life more fulfilling? How can we craft an extraordinary life? Figuring out what we really want to be or do is not as easy as it sounds. Many of us go through life without truly finding much purpose and so end up adrift or in an occupation or job by default.

Unless you have found your life's purpose and mission that provides for you financially, you are *not* what you do. The person you were meant to be is probably still inside you, struggling to manifest itself but held back by the realities of everyday life, turning you into an unhappy and unfulfilled person in the process.

Minimalism helps you to uncover these hidden dreams that hadn't the time, space, or freedom to manifest in your current life. It facilitates deliberate living and constant probing as to what adds value and meaning—and what doesn't. Once you are able to identify what really matters to you, you will realize what you need to do to make space for it, in the process making your life good—extraordinary, even. Then you can let go of everything else, because you will now recognize it as clutter—things that come in the way of the life you are meant to live.

As Kate Carpenter aptly describes in her book *ENUFF*, what you want to *do* will be a verb. What you want to *be* will be an adjective. What you want to *have* will be a noun. So what are you passionate and excited about? What is your purpose and mission? Ultimately, how do you want to feel about your life, and how do you want to derive meaning from it?

One's passion is not predetermined; neither is it permanent, life-long, and limited to a singular pursuit. We can be passionate about anything, as long as it aligns with our beliefs and values. Like our lives, our purposes and passions are open to change and evolvement. To unearth your passion, it is useful to think about the activities that capture and focus your attention so completely that you are totally unaware of your surroundings and the passing of time. That is your passion and purpose, at least for a particular phase in your life.

When you are wholly absorbed in a task, you are doing something where your passions and talents mesh fully and completely. When that happens, you have found your mission. Like passion, your mission is not pre-existing, and it is not always easy to find or pursue. But when you find something—anything—that you are passionate about, and you make it your life's mission, there will be great joy and reward in the work you do. Finding your mission and living it—even if part-time—will allow you to fulfill both your life's purpose and potential, and likely provide you with happiness and fulfillment in the process.

In his book *Flow*, psychologist Mihaly Csikszentmihalyi studied a state of happiness, triggered by concentration, that he termed *flow*. The key to *flow* is the sense of contentment with the passing of time. When one is completely immersed in something (for example, writing or playing music), they lose track of time and tend to forget their problems. This level of immersion is rarely possible until we've reduced or eliminated all distractions and nonessential things, after which *flow* can take place—and that leads to happiness.

I believe that when you do what you love for a living, you are free; when you love what you do for a living, you are happy. People who do what they love for a living tend to refer to their work as their mission. In turn, one's mission is cultivated after many hours of doing the work—never simply discovered or stumbled upon.

My life's purpose is to experience living well with less; and with my passion for minimalist living, my mission is to share my findings with others through my inspired ventures (blog, books, minimalism mentoring).

What's yours?

*My mission in life is not merely to survive, but to thrive; and
to do so with some passion, some compassion,
some humor, and some style.*

—Maya Angelou

Stretching and reaching beyond ourselves

Happiness, as I have experienced personally, is achieved through living a meaningful life. A life that is focused on what is really important and what brings us joy; a life that is filled with freedom and inspiration, in which I can grow as an individual and contribute to other people in meaningful ways.

Growth and contribution—those are the bedrocks of happiness. Not stuff. Without growth and contribution, our lives remain small, and we cease to truly live.

Without stretching ourselves, we don't grow. Without reaching out in a deliberate effort to help others, we are simply living mini-versions of what our life could be; confined within the accepted norms of social and cultural expectations, framed by money, status, and other benchmarks of perceived successes.

The Minimalists have summarized success in a simple equation:

Happiness + Constant Improvement + Contribution
= Success

Life is a lot about taking, but also about giving—just as in yin and yang, our taking and giving must be in balance.

The world becomes a better place when people give as much as they take or, even better, give more than they take. Unfortunately, our current world is out of balance. We waste little time in plundering natural resources and energy, and greed is considered as acceptable or even preferred by certain individuals and groups. A misaligned and unbalanced world is unequivocally not sustainable.

Activity: What can you offer, in whatever way you can, to make this world a better place?

Only those who have learned the power of sincere and selfless contribution experience life's deepest joy: true fulfillment.

—Anthony Robbins

A day in the life of a minimalist

So what is a minimalist life like? Is it any different from the life of one who does not identify as one? I guess the answer is yes and no. Being a minimalist does not exempt one from the ups and downs of daily life. What minimalism does is provide us with a set of beliefs, values, and habits to facilitate more intentional living and help us make more conscious decisions—with the aim of making our lives happier, more fulfilling, and even extraordinary, in one way or more.

An extraordinary life does not just "happen" to us. Like any masterpiece, we need to invest the time and effort to build, craft, and curate it. It involves making more than one life-changing decision. It is a myriad of big and small daily decisions revolving around your beliefs, and what you want to keep and allow into your life, as well as money, health, and growth. These decisions build up to form the basis and constituents of a minimalist life—one that is extraordinary and that we can be proud of.

***

Ever since I left my corporate job and started working on my own businesses, I no longer have a routine that I abide to.

What I have instead are rituals and habits to anchor my day, and I leave the rest to be shaped by inspiration and serendipity.

Here's what a typical day of mine might look like:

Though I tend to be a night owl, I enjoy the benefits of waking up bright and early. It makes my day stretch out much longer, and I feel as if my day has been more productive. Sleep is important to the quality of my day, and I make sure I get at least seven, if not eight hours, every night (gone are the days when I could easily survive on six or less hours!). I have long since given up going to bed at 11 p.m. and expecting to wake at 7 a.m. when my usual sleeping and waking hours are closer to 2 a.m. and 9 a.m.—I am just setting myself up for failure. If I want to get up early, I make it a point to go to bed earlier. What I do is create a habit of getting to bed fifteen minutes earlier and waking up fifteen minutes earlier. Do that for a few days and then get to bed thirty minutes earlier and wake up thirty minutes earlier, and so on. It makes the transition more gradual and doable.

My morning rituals are key to the quality and success of my day. I do five minutes of intentions for my life and the day, followed by ten minutes of exercises. After my shower, I have a small breakfast. I am quite serious about good quality coffee. Making a mindful exercise out of my morning coffee ritual helps me to make better coffee and appreciate my drink even more. I try to be aware of every step of the process, from filling the kettle and scooping the coffee into the filter to taking the first sip and truly appreciating the aroma and depth of taste.

I do my quiet time over coffee—about fifteen minutes of meditation and affirmations in silence. This is followed by about half an hour of writing notes, checking my emails, investments, sorting out a couple of administrative items, and checking out a few key websites. These are my morning rituals that help me to anchor my days. The rest of the day is shaped by the projects I am working on and what I am inspired to do and where I want to be.

When I was working on this book, I would spend the next two hours writing. I was tempted every now and again to check my emails, surf the web, and check out Facebook. Sometimes I managed to focus on the writing, but quite a few times I yielded to my temptations. It took me some time after that to get back into the groove of writing. I tried out the Pomodoro technique—an app that times you so that you work for twenty-five minutes and then break for five minutes—which worked out quite well. It helped me to focus on writing so I could look forward to my five-minute break—either to make a drink or surf the net without guilt. Then it would be back to another twenty-five minutes of work. I am still working on my habit of focusing.

I would then head into town for various errands. Once, I left to check out the venue for the next London Minimalists Meetup, a group that I head. We needed a bigger venue for the next event, when we were expecting an acclaimed author and speaker on the Slow Movement. Since I began my minimalism journey a few years ago, I have benefited so much from this way of living, and heading up the Minimalists Group was my way of giving back. It serves as an excellent platform to meet fellow aspiring and practicing minimalists with similar desires to live well with less.

When I am in Central London, I make an effort to visit two of my favorite places: Foyles Bookshop and the National Gallery. Is no secret that I love books, and I am like a bee to honey when it comes to beautiful bookshops. I still buy books as they give me much joy and inspiration, but I do so with more deliberation and moderation. Unlike in the past, when I usually walked out of a bookshop with a few books, today I tend to buy one book, if I can find the right one, and then finish it before buying the next one. This helps me focus on and appreciate the book I am reading. I guess one can have too much of a good thing, even with books!

That particular day, my purchase was not a book but *Kinfolk*, a beautifully crafted lifestyle magazine that focuses on simplifying lives, cultivating community, and spending time with loved ones. Aptly, the new issue's theme was on essentialism and the celebration of who and what we value most. Indeed, as I read it, I was doing what gives me bliss: poring over a magazine over a cup of coffee and some light lunch at the bookshop café.

I always make it a point to visit the National Gallery for at least half an hour whenever I am in the area. Gone are the days when I would walk past painting after painting and gallery after gallery, wanting to take in all the beauty, but let down by my exhaustion and the overload of imagery. Instead, today I focus on my favorite painters and paintings during my visits. That day, I headed straight for the Canaletto room where his paintings of Venice are unmatchable in their detail and clarity. I took my time looking and appreciating each piece of work. I guess one can never tire of exquisite craftsmanship.

Once I return home, I decide on dinner. I cooked a simple meal of spaghetti with tuna and anchovies that evening, helped along by Dave Brubeck's jazzy notes in the background. For me, it is jazz in summer and classical music in winter. The whole process of preparing a meal—chopping, stirring and cooking—is both meditative and therapeutic, and I take my time. I always believe that food tastes much better when there is love and inspiration involved in its preparation. There is nowhere I need to be, and, as I have no TV, no TV schedule to keep. Dinner time is also when my partner and I catch up on our days and spend some quality time together. The day draws to a close and I read until sleep beckons.

That is my example of a nice day. I did some productive work and visited the bookshop and gallery, which provided much joy and inspiration. It was not too eventful, but there was enough to make it interesting. Most important, it was intentional and well-lived.

When we live minimally, we live more mindfully.

—Francine Jay

Chapter 8:
Closing Thoughts

Key take-outs

* Many of us have not found happiness and fulfillment with being more, having more, and doing more. So embracing minimalism and living well with less might be the answer.
* Being a minimalist is a joy and not a deprivation. It is personal and unmeasurable—the balance between less and more. It is a journey, not a destination.
* Minimalism is about focusing on what provides happiness, value, and purpose. It is about what truly matters to us and what we can't live without—the essentials.
* Anything that is not essential is clutter, which can be physical, mental, or emotional—anything that stands between you and the life you want to live.

- When it comes to separating the essentials from the clutter, always ask, "Does this add value, serve a purpose, or provide happiness?"
- We all have but one life. Have the courage to be your true self. You define what constitutes your own happiness and success.
- The space in your life that is created through minimalism will allow your true purpose, passions, and mission to emerge; and it will also steer you toward more joy, freedom, and meaning—an extraordinary life.
- Living well with less is about experiencing life with more: more happiness, calm, intention, and fulfillment. It is more, with less.

Resources

Websites

- Live Well with Less: livewellwithless.com
- The Story of Stuff: storyofstuff.org

Blogs

- Simple and Minimal: livewellwithless.com/blog
- The Minimalists: theminimalists.com
- Miss Minimalist: missminimalist.com
- Zen Habits: zenhabits.net
- Becoming Minimalist: becomingminimalist.com
- Be More With Less: bemorewithless.com

Notes

Introduction

Pg x: David G. Myers, "The funds, friends, and faith of happy people" *American Psychologist* (Jan 2000, Vol.55, No.1)

Chapter 1

Pg 9: Kate Carpenter, *Enuff* (International: Amazon Publishing, 2012), quote

Pg 11: Dave Bruno, *The Hundred Thing Challenge* (US: William Morrow, 2011), quote

Pg 16: Allen Saunders, "Quotable Quotes" *Readers Digest* (Jan 1957), quote

Chapter 2

Pg 17: James Wallman, *Stuffocation* (UK: Penguin, 2016)

Pg 18: Kat Stoeffel, "You only wear 20% of your wardrobe regularly" *The Cut* (April 2013)

Pg 18: James Wallman, "The hazards of too much stuff" *BBC Magazine* (Jan 2015)

Pg 18: Jeanne E. Arnold, Anthony P. Graesch, Enzo Ragazzini, and Elinor Ochs, *Life at Home in the Twenty-First Century: 32 Families*

Open Their Doors (US: UCLA Cotsen Institute of Archaeology Press, 2012*)*

Pg 19: Jon Mooallem, "The Self-Storage Self," *The New York Times Magazine* (Sept 2009)

Pg 19: Chuck Palahnuik, *Fight Club* (US: W. W. Norton & Co, 1996), quote

Pg 23: Peter Walsh, *It's All Too Much: An Easy Plan for Living a Richer Life with Less Stuff* (UK: Simon & Schuster, 2008), quote

Chapter 3

Pg 26: William Morris, *Hopes and Fears for Art: Five Lectures Delivered in Birmingham, London, and Nottingham, 1878–1881* (1882), quote

Pg 27: Banani Ray and Amit Ray, *Awakening Inner Guru* (International: Inner Light Publishers, 2010), quote

Pg 28: Marie Kondo, *The Life-Changing Magic of Tidying: A simple, effective way to banish clutter forever* (UK: Vermillion, 2014)

Pg 29: Joshua Becker, "Don't just declutter, de-own," *becomingminimalist. com*, quote

Pg 31: Carpenter, *Enuff*, quote

Pg 67: Leo Babauta, *The Power of Less* (UK: Hay House, 2009), quote

Chapter 4

Pg 71: Steve Jobs, Commencement speech at Stanford University (2005), quote

Pg 74: Greg McKeown, *Essentialism: The Disciplined Pursuit of Less* (UK: Virgin Books, 2014), quote

Pg 77: Carl Honoré, *In Praise of Slowness: How a Worldwide Movement is Challenging the Cult of Speed* (US: HarperCollins, 2004), quote

Pg 78: Henry David Thoreau, *Letter to Harrison Blake* (16 November 1857), quote

Pg 82: Timothy Ferriss, *The 4-Hour Work Week: Escape the 9-5, Live Anywhere and Join the New Rich* (UK: Vermillion, 2011), quote

Pg 88: Eckhart Tolle, *The Power of Now* (UK: Yellow Kite, 2011), quote

Pg 95: Tolle, *The Power of Now*

Chapter 5

Pg 108: Joshua Fields Milburn and Ryan Nicodemus (The Minimalists), *Essential: Essays by The Minimalists* (US: Asymmetrical Press, 2012), quote

Pg 109: Ellen Hopkins, *Fallout* (US: Margaret K. McElderry Books, 2013)

Pg 111: Leo Babauta, "Expanding the envelope: A method for beating anger," *zenhabits.net*

Chapter 6

Pg 131: Barack Obama, Inaugural speech on Inauguration Day (January 20, 2009), quote

Pg 133: Milburn and Nicodemus (The Minimalists), *Essential*

Pg 136: Chris Brogan, *Trust Agents: Using the Web to Build Influence, Improve Reputation, and Earn Trust* (UK: John Wiley & Sons, 2010), quote

Pg 138: Oscar Wilde, *The Picture of Dorian Gray* (Lippincott's Monthly Magazine, July 1890), quote

Pg 146: Henry David Thoreau, *Walden* (US: Ticknor and Fields, 1854), quote

Pg 153: Henrik Ibsen, *Prose Dramas* (US: Wildside Press LLC, 2007), quote

Chapter 7

Pg 159: Viktor Frankl, *Man's Search for Meaning: The Classic Tribute to Hope from the Holocaust* (UK: Rider, 2004)

Pg 161: David Viscott, *Finding Your Strength in Difficult Times: A Book of Meditations* (Europe: McGraw-Hill Education, 2003), quote

Pg 163: Carpenter, *Enuff*, quote

Pg 164: Mihaly Csikszentmihalyi, *Flow: The Psychology of Happiness* (UK: Rider, 2002)

Pg 165: Maya Angelou, *Facebook* post (2011), quote

Pg 166: Milburn and Nicodemus (The Minimalists), *Essential*, quote

Pg 167: Anthony Robbins, *Awaken the Giant Within: How to Take Immediate Control of Your Mental, Physical, Emotional and Financial Life* (UK: Simon & Schuster, 2001), quote

Pg 173: Francine Jay, *The Joy of Less* (US: Chronicle Books, 2016), quote